Lysistrata and Other Plays

By Aristophanes

Lysistrata and Other Plays

Published by ReadaClassic.com

TABLE OF CONTENTS

LYSISTRATA

Characters

LYSISTRATA

CLEONICE

MYRRHINE

LAMPITO

MAGISTRATES

CINESIAS

CHILD OF CINESIAS

HERALD OF THE LACEDAEMONIANS

ENVOYS OF THE LACEDAEMONIANS

AN ATHENIAN CITIZEN

CHORUS OF OLD MEN

CHORUS OF WOMEN

THE PLAY

SCENE: At the base of the Orchestra are two buildings, the house of LYSISTRATA: and the entrance to the Acropolis; a winding and narrow path leads up to the latter. Between the two buildings is the opening of the Cave of Pan. LYSISTRATA: is pacing up and down in front of her house.

LYSISTRATA: Ah! if only they had been invited to a Bacchic revelling, or a feast of Pan or Aphrodite or Genetyllis, why! the streets would have been impassable for the thronging tambourines! Now there's never a woman here-ah! except my neighbour Cleonice, whom I see approaching yonder.... Good day, Cleonice.

CLEONICE: Good day, Lysistrata; but pray, why this dark, forbidding face, my dear? Believe me, you don't look a bit pretty with those black lowering brows.

LYSISTRATA: Oh, Cleonice, my heart is on fire; I blush for our sex. Men will have it we are tricky and sly....

CLEONICE: And they are quite right, upon my word!

LYSISTRATA: Yet, look you, when the women are summoned to meet for a matter of the greatest importance, they lie in bed instead of coming.

CLEONICE: Oh! they will come, my dear; but it's not easy, you know, for women to leave the house. One is busy pottering about her husband; another is getting the servant up; a third is putting her child asleep or washing the brat or feeding it.

LYSISTRATA: But I tell you, the business that calls them here is far and away more urgent.

CLEONICE: And why do you summon us, dear Lysistrata? What is it all about?

LYSISTRATA: About a big thing.

5

CLEONICE (taking this in a different sense; with great interest): And is it thick too?

LYSISTRATA: Yes, very thick.

CLEONICE: And we are not all on the spot! Imagine!

LYSISTRATA (wearily): Oh! if it were what you suppose, there would be never an absentee. No, no, it concerns a thing I have turned about and about this way and that so many sleepless nights.

CLEONICE (still unable to be serious): It must be something mighty fine and subtle for you to have turned it about so!

LYSISTRATA: So fine, it means just this, Greece saved by the women!

CLEONICE: By the women! Why, its salvation hangs on a poor thread then!
LYSISTRATA: Our country's fortunes depend on us-it is with us to undo utterly the Peloponnesians.

CLEONICE: That would be a noble deed truly!

LYSISTRATA: To exterminate the Boeotians to a man!

CLEONICE: But surely you would spare the eels.

LYSISTRATA: For Athens' sake I will never threaten so fell a doom; trust me for that. However, if the Boeotian and Peloponnesian women join us, Greece is saved.

CLEONICE: But how should women perform so wise and glorious an achievement, we women who dwell in the retirement of the household, clad in diaphanous garments of yellow silk and long flowing gowns, decked out with flowers and shod with dainty little slippers?

6

LYSISTRATA: Ah, but those are the very sheet-anchors of our salvation-those yellow tunics, those scents and slippers, those cosmetics and transparent robes.

CLEONICE: How so, pray?

LYSISTRATA: There is not a man will wield a lance against another...

CLEONICE: Quick, I will get me a yellow tunic from the dyer's.

LYSISTRATA: ...or want a shield.

CLEONICE: I'll run and put on a flowing gown.

LYSISTRATA: ...or draw a sword.

CLEONICE: I'll haste and buy a pair of slippers this instant.

LYSISTRATA: Now tell me, would not the women have done best to come?

CLEONICE: Why, they should have flown here!

LYSISTRATA: Ah! my dear, you'll see that like true Athenians, they will do everything too late.... Why, there's not a woman come from the shore, not one from Salamis.

CLEONICE: But I know for certain they embarked at daybreak.

LYSISTRATA: And the dames from Acharnae! why, I thought they would have been the very first to arrive.

CLEONICE: Theagenes' wife at any rate is sure to come; she has actually been to consult Hecate.... But look! here are some arrivals-and there are more behind. Ah! ha! now what countrywomen may they be?

LYSISTRATA: They are from Anagyra.

CLEONICE: Yes! upon my word, 'tis a levy en masse of all the female population of Anagyra!
(MYRRHINE: enters, followed by other women.)

MYRRHINE: Are we late, Lysistrata? Tell us, pray; what, not a word?

LYSISTRATA: I cannot say much for you, Myrrhine! you have not bestirred yourself overmuch for an affair of such urgency.

MYRRHINE: I could not find my girdle in the dark. However, if the matter is so pressing, here we are; so speak.

CLEONICE: No, let's wait a moment more, till the women of Boeotia arrive and those from the Peloponnese.

LYSISTRATA: Yes, that is best.... Ah! here comes Lampito. (LAMPITO, a husky Spartan damsel, enters with three others, two from Boeotia and one from Corinth.) Good day, Lampito, dear friend from Lacedaemon. How well and handsome you look! what a rosy complexion! and how strong you seem; why, you could strangle a bull surely!

LAMPITO: Yes, indeed, I really think I could. It's because I do gymnastics and practice the bottom-kicking dance.

CLEONICE (opening LAMPITO'S robe and baring her bosom): And what superb breasts!

LAMPITO: La! you are feeling me as if I were a beast for sacrifice.

LYSISTRATA: And this young woman, where is she from?
LAMPITO: She is a noble lady from Boeotia.

LYSISTRATA: Ah! my pretty Boeotian friend, you are as blooming as a garden.

8

CLEONICE (making another inspection): Yes, on my word! and her "garden" is so thoroughly weeded too!

LYSISTRATA (pointing to the Corinthian): And who is this?

LAMPITO: 'Tis an honest woman, by my faith! she comes from Corinth.

CLEONICE: Oh! honest, no doubt then-as honesty goes at Corinth.

LAMPITO: But who has called together this council of women, pray?

LYSISTRATA: I have.

LAMPITO: Well then, tell us what you want of us.

CLEONICE: Yes, please tell us! What is this very important business you wish to inform us about?

LYSISTRATA: I will tell you. But first answer me one question.

CLEONICE: Anything you wish.

LYSISTRATA: Don't you feel sad and sorry because the fathers of your children are far away from you with the army? For I'll wager there is not one of you whose husband is not abroad at this moment.

CLEONICE: Mine has been the last five months in Thrace-looking after Eucrates.

MYRRHINE: It's seven long months since mine left for Pylos.

LAMPITO: As for mine, if he ever does return from service, he's no sooner home than he takes down his shield again and flies back to the wars.

LYSISTRATA: And not so much as the shadow of a lover! Since the day the Milesians betrayed us, I have never once seen an eight-inch gadget even, to be a

9

leathern consolation to us poor widows.... Now tell me, if I have discovered a means of ending the war, will you all second me?

CLEONICE: Yes verily, by all the goddesses, I swear I will, though I have to put my gown in pawn, and drink the money the same day.

MYRRHINE: And so will I, though I must be split in two like a flat-fish, and have half myself removed.

LAMPITO: And I too; why to secure peace, I would climb to the top of Mount Taygetus.

LYSISTRATA: Then I will out with it at last, my mighty secret!
Oh! sister women, if we would compel our husbands to make peace, we must refrain...

CLEONICE: Refrain from what? tell us, tell us!

LYSISTRATA: But will you do it?

MYRRHINE: We will, we will, though we should die of it.

LYSISTRATA: We must refrain from the male altogether.... Nay, why do you turn your backs on me? Where are you going? So, you bite your lips, and shake your heads, eh? Why these pale, sad looks? why these tears? Come, will you do it-yes or no? Do you hesitate?

CLEONICE: I will not do it, let the war go on.

MYRRHINE: Nor will I; let the war go on.

LYSISTRATA (to MYRRHINE): And you say this, my pretty flat-fish, who declared just now they might split you in two?

CLEONICE: Anything, anything but that! Bid me go through the fire, if you will, but to rob us of the sweetest thing in all the world, LYSISTRATA darling!

LYSISTRATA (to MYRRHINE): And you?

MYRRHINE: Yes, I agree with the others; I too would sooner go through the fire.

LYSISTRATA: Oh, wanton, vicious sex! The poets have done well to make tragedies upon us; we are good for nothing then but love and lewdness! But you, my dear, you from hardy Sparta, if you join me, all may yet be well; help me, second me, I beg you.

LAMPITO: 'Tis a hard thing, by the two goddesses it is! for a woman to sleep alone without ever a strong male in her bed. But there, peace must come first.

LYSISTRATA: Oh, my darling, my dearest, best friend, you are the only one deserving the name of woman!

CLEONICE: But if—which the gods forbid—we do refrain altogether from what you say, should we get peace any sooner?

LYSISTRATA: Of course we should, by the goddesses twain! We need only sit indoors with painted cheeks, and meet our mates lightly clad in transparent gowns of Amorgos silk, and perfectly depilated; they will get their tools up and be wild to lie with us. That will be the time to refuse, and they will hasten to make peace, I am convinced of that!

LAMPITO: Yes, just as Menelaus, when he saw Helen's naked bosom, threw away his sword, they say.

CLEONICE: But, oh dear, suppose our husbands go away and leave us.

LYSISTRATA: Then, as Pherecrates says, we must "flay a skinned dog," that's all.
CLEONICE: Fiddlesticks! these proverbs are all idle talk.... But if our husbands drag us by main force into the bedchamber?

LYSISTRATA: Hold on to the door posts. But if they beat us?

LYSISTRATA: Then yield to their wishes, but with a bad grace; there is no pleasure in it for them, when they do it by force. Besides, there are a thousand ways of tormenting them. Never fear, they'll soon tire of the game; there's no satisfaction for a man, unless the woman shares it.

CLEONICE: Very well, if you must have it so, we agree.

LAMPITO: For ourselves, no doubt we shall persuade our husbands to conclude a fair and honest peace; but there is the Athenian populace, how are we to cure these folk of their warlike frenzy?

LYSISTRATA: Have no fear; we undertake to make our own people listen to reason.

LAMPITO: That's impossible, so long as they have their trusty ships and the vast treasures stored in the temple of Athene.

LYSISTRATA: Ah! but we have seen to that; this very day the Acropolis will be in our hands. That is the task assigned to the older women; while we are here in council, they are going, under pretence of offering sacrifice, to seize the citadel.

LAMPITO: Well said indeed! everything is going for the best.
LYSISTRATA: Come, quick, Lampito, and let us bind ourselves by an inviolable oath.

LAMPITO: Recite the terms; we will swear to them.

LYSISTRATA: With pleasure. Where is our Scythian policewoman? Now, what are you staring at, pray? Lay this shield on the earth before us, its hollow upwards, and someone bring me the victim's inwards.

CLEONICE: Lysistrata, say, what oath are we to swear?

LYSISTRATA: What oath? Why, in Aeschylus, they sacrifice a sheep, and swear over a buckler; we will do the same.

CLEONICE: No, Lysistrata, one cannot swear peace over a buckler, surely.

LYSISTRATA: What other oath do you prefer?

CLEONICE: Let's take a white horse, and sacrifice it, and swear on its entrails.

LYSISTRATA: But where shall we get a white horse?

CLEONICE: Well, what oath shall we take then?

LYSISTRATA: Listen to me. Let's set a great black bowl on the ground; let's sacrifice a skin of Thasian wine into it, and take oath not to add one single drop of water.

LAMPITO: Ah! that's an oath pleases me more than I can say.

LYSISTRATA: Let them bring me a bowl and a skin of wine.

CLEONICE: Ah! my dears, what a noble big bowl! what fun it will be to empty it.

LYSISTRATA: Set the bowl down on the ground, and lay your hands on the victim. ....Almighty goddess, Persuasion, and thou, bowl, boon comrade of joy and merriment, receive this our sacrifice, and be propitious to us poor women!

CLEONICE (as LYSISTRATA: pours the wine into the bowl): Oh! the fine red blood! how well it flows!

LAMPITO: And what a delicious bouquet, by Castor!

CLEONICE: Now, my dears, let me swear first, if you please.

LYSISTRATA: No, by Aphrodite, unless it's decided by lot. But come, then, Lampito, and all of you, put your hands to the bowl; and do you, Cleonice, repeat for all the rest the solemn terms I am going to recite. Then you must all swear, and pledge yourselves by the same promises,-I will have naught to do whether with lover or husband...

CLEONICE (faintly): I will have naught to do whether with lover or husband...

LYSISTRATA: Albeit he come to me with an erection...

CLEONICE (her voice quavering): Albeit he come to me with an erection... (in despair) Oh! Lysistrata, I cannot bear it!

LYSISTRATA (ignoring this outburst): I will live at home unbulled...

CLEONICE: I will live at home unbulled...

LYSISTRATA: Beautifully dressed and wearing a saffron-coloured gown

CLEONICE: Beautifully dressed and wearing a saffron-coloured gown...

LYSISTRATA: To the end I may inspire my husband with the most ardent longings.

CLEONICE: To the end I may inspire my husband with the most ardent longings.

LYSISTRATA: Never will I give myself voluntarily...

CLEONICE: Never will I give myself voluntarily...

LYSISTRATA: And if he has me by force...

CLEONICE: And if he has me by force...

LYSISTRATA: I will be cold as ice, and never stir a limb...

14

CLEONICE: I will be cold as ice, and never stir a limb...

LYSISTRATA: I will neither extend my Persian slippers toward the ceiling...

CLEONICE: I will neither extend my Persian slippers toward the ceiling...

LYSISTRATA: Nor will I crouch like the carven lions on a knife-handle.

CLEONICE: Nor will I crouch like the carven lions on a knife-handle.

LYSISTRATA: And if I keep my oath, may I be suffered to drink of this wine.

CLEONICE (more courageously): And if I keep my oath, may I be suffered to drink of this wine.

LYSISTRATA: But if I break it, let my bowl be filled with water.

CLEONICE: But if I break it, let my bowl be filled with water.

LYSISTRATA: Will you all take this oath?

ALL: We do.

LYSISTRATA: Then I'll now consume this remnant. (She drinks.)

CLEONICE (reaching for the cup): Enough, enough, my dear; now let us all drink in turn to cement our friendship.

(They pass the cup around and all drink. A great commotion is heard off stage.)

LAMPITO: Listen! what do those cries mean?

LYSISTRATA: It's what I was telling you; the women have just occupied the Acropolis. So now, Lampito, you return to Sparta to organize the plot, while your

15

comrades here remain as hostages. For ourselves, let us go and join the rest in the citadel, and let us push the bolts well home.

CLEONICE: But don't you think the men will march up against us?

LYSISTRATA: I laugh at them. Neither threats nor flames shall force our doors; they shall open only on the conditions I have named.

CLEONICE: Yes, yes, by Aphrodite; otherwise we should be called cowardly and wretched women.

(She follows LYSISTRATA: out.)

(The scene shifts to the entrance of the Acropolis. The CHORUS OF OLD MEN: slowly enters, carrying faggots and pots of fire.)

LEADER OF CHORUS OF OLD MEN: Go easy, Draces, go easy; why, your shoulder is all chafed by these damned heavy olive stocks. But forward still, forward, man, as needs must.

FIRST SEMI-CHORUS OF OLD MEN (singing): What unlooked-for things do happen, to be sure, in a long life! Ah! Strymodorus, who would ever have thought it? Here we have the women, who used, for our misfortune, to eat our bread and live in our houses, daring nowadays to lay hands on the holy image of the goddess, to seize the Acropolis and draw bars and bolts to keep any from entering!

LEADER OF CHORUS OF OLD MEN: Come, Philurgus, man, let's hurry there; let's lay our faggots all about the citadel, and on the blazing pile burn with our hands these vile conspiratresses, one and all-and Lycon's wife first and foremost!

SECOND SEMI-CHORUS OF OLD MEN (singing): Nay, by Demeter, never will I let them laugh at me, whiles I have a breath left in my body. Cleomenes himself, the first who ever seized our citadel, had to quit it to his sore dishonour; spite his Lacedaemonian pride, he had to deliver me up his arms and slink off with a single garment to his back. My word! but he was filthy and ragged! and what an unkempt beard, to be sure! He had not had a bath for six long years!

LEADER OF CHORUS OF OLD MEN: Oh! but that was a mighty siege! Our men were ranged seventeen deep before the gate, and never left their posts, even to sleep. These women, these enemies of Euripides and all the gods, shall I do nothing to hinder their inordinate insolence? else let them tear down my trophies of Marathon.

FIRST SEMI-CHORUS OF OLD MEN (singing): But look, to finish this toilsome climb only this last steep bit is left to mount. Truly, it's no easy job without beasts of burden, and how these logs do bruise my shoulder! Still let us carry on, and blow up our fire and see it does not go out just as we reach our destination. Phew! phew! (Blowing the fire) Oh! dear! what a dreadful smoke!

SECOND SEMI-CHORUS OF OLD MEN (singing): It bites my eyes like a mad dog. It is Lemnian fire for sure, or it would never devour my eyelids like this. Come on, Laches, let's hurry, let's bring succour to the goddess; it's now or never! Phew! phew! (Blowing the fire) Oh dear! what a confounded smoke!

LEADER OF CHORUS OF OLD MEN: There now, there's our fire all bright and burning, thank the gods! Now, why not first put down our loads here, then take a vine-branch, light it at the brazier and hurl it at the gate by way of battering-ram? If they don't answer our summons by pulling back the bolts, then we set fire to the woodwork, and the smoke will choke them. Ye gods! what a smoke! Pfaugh! Is there never a Samian general will help me unload my burden?-Ah! it shall not gall my shoulder any more. (Setting down the wood) Come, brazier, do your duty, make the embers flare, that I may kindle a brand; I want to be the first to hurl one. Aid me, heavenly Victory; let us punish for their insolent audacity the women who have seized our citadel, and may we raise a trophy of triumph for success!

(They begin to build a fire. The CHORUS OF WOMEN: now enters, carrying pots of water.)

LEADER OF CHORUS OF WOMEN: Oh! my dears, methinks I see fire and smoke; can it be a conflagration? Let us
hurry all we can.

FIRST SEMI-CHORUS OF WOMEN (singing): Fly, fly, Nicodice, ere Calyce and Critylle perish in the fire, or are stifled in the smoke raised by these accursed old men and their pitiless laws. But, great gods, can it be I come too late? Rising at dawn, I had the utmost trouble to fill this vessel at the fountain. Oh! what a crowd there was, and what a din! What a rattling of water-pots! Servants and slave-girls pushed and thronged me! However, here I have it full at last; and I am running to carry the water to my fellow-townswomen, whom our foes are plotting to burn alive.

SECOND SEMI-CHORUS OF WOMEN (singing): News has been brought us that a company of old, doddering grey-beards, loaded with enormous faggots, as if they wanted to heat a furnace, have taken the field, vomiting dreadful threats, crying that they must reduce to ashes these horrible women. Suffer them not, oh! goddess, but, of thy grace, may I see Athens and Greece cured of their warlike folly. 'Tis to this end, oh! thou guardian deity of our city, goddess of the golden crest, that they have seized thy sanctuary. Be their friend and ally, Athene, and if any man hurl against them lighted firebrands, aid us to carry water to extinguish them.

LEADER OF CHORUS OF WOMEN: What is this I see, ye wretched old men? Honest and pious folk ye cannot be who act so vilely.

LEADER OF CHORUS OF OLD MEN: Ah, ha! here's something new! a swarm of women stand posted outside to defend the gates!
LEADER OF CHORUS OF WOMEN: Fart at us, would you? we seem a mighty host, yet you do not see the ten-thousandth part of our sex.

LEADER OF CHORUS OF OLD MEN: Ho, Phaedrias! shall we stop their cackle? Suppose one of us were to break a stick across their backs, eh?

LEADER OF CHORUS OF WOMEN: Let us set down our water-pots on the ground, to be out of the way, if they should dare to offer us violence.

18

LEADER OF CHORUS OF OLD MEN: Let someone knock out two or three teeth for them, as they did to Bupalus; they won't talk so loud then.

LEADER OF CHORUS OF WOMEN: Come on then; I wait you with unflinching foot, and no other bitch will ever grab your balls.

LEADER OF CHORUS OF OLD MEN: Silence! or my stick will cut short your days.

LEADER OF CHORUS OF WOMEN: Now, just you dare to touch Stratyllis with the tip of your finger!

LEADER OF CHORUS OF OLD MEN: And if I batter you to pieces with my fists, what will you do?

LEADER OF CHORUS OF WOMEN: I will tear out your lungs and entrails with my teeth.

LEADER OF CHORUS OF OLD MEN: Oh! what a clever poet is Euripides! how well he says that woman is the most shameless of animals.

LEADER OF CHORUS OF WOMEN: Let's pick up our water-jars again, Rhodippe.

LEADER OF CHORUS OF OLD MEN: You damned women, what do you mean to do here with your water?

LEADER OF CHORUS OF WOMEN: And you, old death-in-life, with your fire? Is it to cremate yourself?

LEADER OF CHORUS OF OLD MEN: I am going to build you a pyre to roast your female friends upon.

LEADER OF CHORUS OF WOMEN: And I, I am going to put out your fire.

LEADER OF CHORUS OF OLD MEN: You put out my fire-you?

LEADER OF CHORUS OF WOMEN: Yes, you shall soon see.

LEADER OF CHORUS OF OLD MEN: I don't know what prevents me from roasting you with this torch.

LEADER OF CHORUS OF WOMEN: I am getting you a bath ready to clean off the filth.

LEADER OF CHORUS OF OLD MEN: A bath for me, you dirty slut?

LEADER OF CHORUS OF WOMEN: Yes, indeed, a nuptial bath-tee heel.

LEADER OF CHORUS OF OLD MEN: (turning to his followers): Do you hear that? What insolence!

LEADER OF CHORUS OF WOMEN: I am a free woman, I tell you.

LEADER OF CHORUS OF OLD MEN: I will make you hold your tongue, never fear!

LEADER OF CHORUS OF WOMEN: Ah ha! you shall never sit any more amongst the Heliasts.

LEADER OF CHORUS OF OLD MEN (to his torch): Burn off her hair for her!

LEADER OF CHORUS OF WOMEN: (to her pot): Achelous, do your duty!

(The women pitch the water in their water-pots over the old men.)

LEADER OF CHORUS OF OLD MEN: Oh, dear! oh, dear! oh, dear!

LEADER OF CHORUS OF WOMEN: Was it hot?

LEADER OF CHORUS OF OLD MEN: Hot, great gods! Enough, enough!

20

LEADER OF CHORUS OF WOMEN: I'm watering you, to make you bloom afresh.

LEADER OF CHORUS OF OLD MEN: Alas! I am too dry! Ah, me how! how I am trembling with cold!

(A MAGISTRATE: enters, with a few Scythian policemen.)

MAGISTRATE: These women, have they made din enough, I wonder, with their tambourines? bewept Adonis enough upon their terraces? I was listening to the speeches last assembly day, and Demostratus, whom heaven confound! was saying we must all go over to Sicily-and lo! his wife was dancing round repeating: "Alas! alas! Adonis, woe is me for Adonis!" Demostratus was saying we must levy hoplites at Zacynthus-and there was his wife, more than half drunk, screaming on the house-roof: "Weep, weep for Adonis!"-while that infamous Mad Ox was bellowing away on his side.-Do you not blush, you women, for your wild and uproarious doings?

LEADER OF CHORUS OF OLD MEN: But you don't know all their effrontery yet! They abused and insulted us; then soused us with the water in their water-pots, and have set us wringing out our clothes, for all the world as if we had be pissed ourselves.

MAGISTRATE: And well done too, by Posidon! We men must share the blame of their ill conduct; it is we who teach them to love riot and dissoluteness and sow the seeds of wickedness in their hearts. You see a husband go into a shop: "Look you, jeweller," says he, "you remember the necklace you made for my wife. well, the other evening, when she was dancing, the catch came open. Now, I am bound to start for Salamis; will you make it convenient to go up to-night to make her fastening secure?" Another will go to the cobbler, a great, strong fellow, with a great, long tool, and tell him: "The strap of one of my wife's sandals presses her little toe, which is extremely sensitive; come in about midday to supple the thing and stretch it." Now see the results. Take my own case-as a MAGISTRATE: I have enlisted rowers; I want money to pay them, and the women slam the door in my face. But why do we stand here with arms crossed? Bring me a crowbar; I'll chastise their insolence!-Ho! there, my fine fellow! (to one of the Scythians) what are, you gaping at the crows for? looking for a tavern, I suppose, eh? Come on, bring crowbars here, and force open the gates. I will put a hand to the work myself.

LYSISTRATA (opening the gate and walking out): No need to force the gates; I am coming out-here I am. And why bolts and bars? What we want here is not bolts and bars and locks, but common sense.

MAGISTRATE (jumping nervously, then striving manfully to regain his dignity): Really, my fine lady! Where is my officer? I want him to tie that woman's hands behind her back.

LYSISTRATA: By Artemis, the virgin goddess! if he touches me with the tip of his finger, officer of the public peace though he be, let him look out for himself! (The first Scythian defecates in terror.)

MAGISTRATE: (to another officer): How now, are you afraid? Seize her, I tell you, round the body. Two of you at her, and have done with it!

CLEONICE: By Pandrosos! if you lay a hand on her, Ill trample you underfoot till the crap comes out of you!

(The second Scythian defecates in terror.)

MAGISTRATE: Look at the mess you've made! Where is there another officer?

(To the third Scythian) Bind that minx first, the one who speaks so prettily!

MYRRHINE: By Phoebe, if you touch her with one finger, you'd better call quick for a surgeon! (The third Scythian defecates in terror.)

MAGISTRATE: What's that? Where's the officer? (To the fourth Scythian) Lay hold of her. Oh! but I'm going to stop your foolishness for you all

CLEONICE: By the Tauric Artemis, if you go near her, I'll pull out your hair, scream as you like.

(The fourth Scythian defecates in terror.)

MAGISTRATE: Ah! miserable man that I am! My own officers desert me. What ho! are we to let ourselves be bested by a mob of women? Ho! Scythians mine, close up your ranks, and forward!

LYSISTRATA: By the holy goddesses! you'll have to make acquaintance with four companies of women, ready for the fray and well armed to boot.

MAGISTRATE: Forward, Scythians, and bind them!

(The Scythians advance reluctantly.)

LYSISTRATA: Forward, my gallant companions; march forth, ye vendors of grain and eggs, garlic and vegetables, keepers of taverns and bakeries, wrench and strike and tear; come, a torrent of invective and insult! (They beat the Scythians who retire in haste.) Enough, enough now retire, never rob the vanquished!

(The women withdraw.)

MAGISTRATE: How unfortunate for my officers!

LYSISTRATA: Ah, ha! so you thought you had only to do with a set of slave-women! you did not know the ardour that fills the bosom of free-born dames.

MAGISTRATE: Ardour! yes, by Apollo, ardour enough-especially for the wine-cup!

LEADER OF CHORUS OF OLD MEN: Sir, sir what good are words? they are of no avail with wild beasts of this sort. Don't you know how they have just washed us down-and with no very fragrant soap!

LEADER OF CHORUS OF WOMEN: What would you have? You should never have laid rash hands on us. If you start afresh, I'll knock your eyes out. My delight is to stay at home as coy as a young MAID: , without hurting anybody or moving any more than a milestone; but 'ware the wasps, if you go stirring up the wasps' nest!

CHORUS OF OLD MEN (singing): Ah! great gods! how get the better of these ferocious creatures? 'tis past all bearing! But come, let us try to find out the reason of the dreadful scourge. With what end in view have they seized the citadel of Cranaus, the sacred shrine that is raised upon the inaccessible rock of the Acropolis?

LEADER OF CHORUS OF OLD MEN (to the MAGISTRATE): Question them; be cautious and not too credulous. It would be culpable negligence not to pierce the mystery, if we may.

MAGISTRATE (addressing the women): I would ask you first why you have barred our gates.

LYSISTRATA: To seize the treasury; no more money, no more war.

MAGISTRATE: Then money is the cause of the war?

LYSISTRATA: And of all our troubles. It was to find occasion to steal that Pisander and all the other agitators were forever raising revolutions. Well and good! but they'll never get another drachma here.

MAGISTRATE: What do you propose to do then, pray?

LYSISTRATA: You ask me that! Why, we propose to administer the treasury ourselves.

MAGISTRATE: You do?

LYSISTRATA: What is there in that to surprise you? Do we not administer the budget of household expenses?

24

MAGISTRATE: But that is not the same thing.

LYSISTRATA: How so—not the same thing?

MAGISTRATE: It is the treasury supplies the expenses of the war.

LYSISTRATA: That's our first principle-no war!

MAGISTRATE: What! and the safety of the city?

LYSISTRATA: We will provide for that.

MAGISTRATE: You?

LYSISTRATA: Yes, we!

MAGISTRATE: What a sorry business!

LYSISTRATA: Yes, we're going to save you, whether you like it or not.

MAGISTRATE: Oh! the impudence of the creatures!

LYSISTRATA: You seem annoyed! but it has to be done, nevertheless.

MAGISTRATE: But it's the very height of iniquity!

LYSISTRATA (testily): We're going to save you, my good man.
MAGISTRATE: But if I don't want to be saved?

LYSISTRATA: Why, all the more reason!

MAGISTRATE: But what a notion, to concern yourselves with questions of peace and war!

LYSISTRATA: We will explain our idea.

25

MAGISTRATE: Out with it then; quick, or... (threatening her).

LYSISTRATA (sternly): Listen, and never a movement, please!

MAGISTRATE (in impotent rage): Oh! it is too much for me! I cannot keep my temper!

LEADER OF CHORUS OF WOMEN: Then look out for yourself; you have more to fear than we have.

MAGISTRATE: Stop your croaking, you old crow! (To LYSISTRATA) Now you, say what you have to say.

LYSISTRATA: Willingly. All the long time the war has lasted, we have endured in modest silence all you men did; you never allowed us to open our lips. We were far from satisfied, for we knew how things were going; often in our homes we would hear you discussing, upside down and inside out, some important turn of affairs. Then with sad hearts, but smiling lips, we would ask you: Well, in today's Assembly did they vote peace?-But, "Mind your own business!" the husband would growl, "Hold your tongue, please!" And we would say no more.

CLEONICE: I would not have held my tongue though, not I!

MAGISTRATE: You would have been reduced to silence by blows then.

LYSISTRATA: Well, for my part, I would say no more. But presently I would come to know you had arrived at some fresh decision more fatally foolish than ever. "Ah! my dear man," I would say, "what madness next!" But he would only look at me askance and say: "Just weave your web, please; else your cheeks will smart for hours. War is men's business!"

MAGISTRATE: Bravo! well said indeed!

LYSISTRATA: How now, wretched man? not to let us contend against your follies was bad enough! But presently we heard you asking out loud in the open street: "Is there never a man left in Athens?" and, "No, not one, not one," you were assured in reply. Then, then we made up our minds without more delay to make common cause to save Greece. Open your ears to our wise counsels and hold your tongues, and we may yet put things on a better footing.

MAGISTRATE: You put things indeed! Oh! this is too much! The insolence of the creatures!

LYSISTRATA: Be still!

MAGISTRATE: May I die a thousand deaths ere I obey one who wears a veil!

LYSISTRATA: If that's all that troubles you, here, take my veil, wrap it round your head, and hold your tongue.

CLEONICE: Then take this basket; put on a girdle, card wool, munch beans. The war shall be women's business.

LEADER OF CHORUS OF WOMEN: Lay aside your water-pots, we will guard them, we will help our friends and companions.

CHORUS OF WOMEN (singing): For myself, I will never weary of the dance; my knees will never grow stiff with fatigue. I will brave everything with my dear allies, on whom Nature has lavished virtue, grace, boldness, cleverness, and whose wisely directed energy is going to save the State.

LEADER OF CHORUS OF WOMEN: Oh! my good, gallant Lysistrata, and all my friends, be ever like a bundle of nettles; never let your anger slacken; the winds of fortune blow our way.

LYSISTRATA: May gentle Love and the sweet Cyprian Queen shower seductive charms on our breasts and our thighs. If only we may stir so amorous a feeling among the men that they stand as firm as sticks, we shall indeed deserve the name of peace-makers among the Greeks.

MAGISTRATE: How will that be, pray?

LYSISTRATA: To begin with, we shall not see you any more running like mad fellows to the Market holding lance in fist.

CLEONICE: That will be something gained, anyway, by the Paphian goddess, it will!

LYSISTRATA: Now we see them, mixed up with saucepans and kitchen stuff, armed to the teeth, looking like wild Corybantes!

MAGISTRATE: Why, of course; that's what brave men should do.

LYSISTRATA: Oh! but what a funny sight, to behold a man wearing a Gorgon's-bead buckler coming along to buy fish!

CLEONICE: The other day in the Market I saw a phylarch with flowing ringlets; he was on horseback, and was pouring into his helmet the broth he had just bought at an old dame's still. There was a Thracian warrior too, who was brandishing his lance like Tereus in the play; he had scared a good woman selling figs into a perfect panic, and was gobbling up all her ripest fruit.

MAGISTRATE: And how, pray, would you propose to restore peace and order in all the countries of Greece?

LYSISTRATA: It's the easiest thing in the world!

MAGISTRATE: Come, tell us how; I am curious to know.

LYSISTRATA: When we are winding thread, and it is tangled, we pass the spool across and through the skein, now this way, now that way; even so, to finish of the war, we shall send embassies hither and thither and everywhere, to disentangle matters.

MAGISTRATE: And is it with your yarn, and your skeins, and your spools, you think to appease so many bitter enmities, you silly women?

LYSISTRATA: If only you had common sense, you would always do in politics the same as we do with our yarn.

MAGISTRATE: Come, how is that, eh?

LYSISTRATA: First we wash the yarn to separate the grease and filth; do the same with all bad citizens, sort them out and drive them forth with rods-they're the refuse of the city. Then for all such as come crowding up in search of employments and offices, we must card them thoroughly; then, to bring them all to the same standard, pitch them pell-mell into the same basket, resident aliens or no, allies, debtors to the State, all mixed up together. Then as for our Colonies, you must think of them as so many isolated hanks; find the ends of the separate threads, draw them to a centre here, wind them into one, make one great hank of the lot, out of which the public can weave itself a good, stout tunic.

MAGISTRATE: Is it not a sin and a shame to see them carding and winding the State, these women who have neither art nor part in the burdens of the war?

LYSISTRATA: What! wretched man! why, it's a far heavier burden to us than to you. In the first place, we bear sons who go off to fight far away from Athens.

MAGISTRATE: Enough said! do not recall sad and sorry memories!

LYSISTRATA: Then secondly, instead of enjoying the pleasures of love and making the best of our youth and beauty, we are left to languish far from our husbands, who are all with the army. But say no more of ourselves; what afflicts me is to see our girls growing old in lonely grief.

MAGISTRATE: Don't the men grow old too?

LYSISTRATA: That is not the same thing. When the soldier returns from the wars, even though he has white hair, he very soon finds a young wife. But a woman has only one summer; if she does not make hay while the sun shines, no one will afterwards have anything to say to her, and she spends her days consulting oracles that never send her a husband.

29

MAGISTRATE: But the old man who can still get an erection...

LYSISTRATA: But you, why don't you get done with it and die? You are rich; go buy yourself a bier, and I will knead you a honey-cake for Cerberus. Here, take this garland.

(Drenching him with water.)

CLEONICE: And this one too.

(Drenching him with water.)

MYRRHINE: And these fillets.
(Drenching him with water.)

LYSISTRATA: What else do you need? Step aboard the boat; Charon is waiting for you, you're keeping him from pushing off.

MAGISTRATE: To treat me so scurvily! What an insult! I will go show myself to my fellow magistrates just as I am.

LYSISTRATA: What! are you blaming us for not having exposed you according to custom? Nay, console yourself; we will not fail to offer up the third-day sacrifice for you, first thing in the morning.

(She goes into the Acropolis, with CLEONICE and MYRRHINE.)

LEADER OF CHORUS OF OLD MEN: Awake, friends of freedom; let us hold ourselves aye ready to act.

CHORUS OF OLD MEN (singing): I suspect a mighty peril; I foresee another tyranny like Hippias'. I am sore afraid the Laconians assembled here with Clisthenes have, by a stratagem of war, stirred up these women, enemies of the gods, to seize upon our treasury and the funds whereby I lived.

LEADER OF CHORUS OF OLD MEN: Is it not a sin and a shame for them to interfere in advising the citizens, to prate of shields and lances, and to ally themselves with Laconians, fellows I trust no more than I would so many famished wolves? The whole thing, my friends, is nothing else but an attempt to re-establish tyranny. But I will never submit; I will be on my guard for the future; I will always carry a blade hidden under myrtle boughs; I will post myself in the public square under arms, shoulder to shoulder with Aristogiton; and now, to make a start, I must just break a few of that cursed old jade's teeth yonder.

LEADER OF CHORUS OF WOMEN: Nay, never play the brave man, else when you go back home, your own mother won't know you. But, dear friends and allies, first let us lay our burdens down.

CHORUS OF WOMEN (singing): Then, citizens all, hear what I have to say. I have useful counsel to give our city, which deserves it well at my hands for the brilliant distinctions it has lavished on my girlhood. At seven years of age, I carried the sacred vessels; at ten, I pounded barley for the altar of Athene; next, clad in a robe of yellow silk, I played the bear to Artemis at the Brauronia; presently, when I was grown up, a tall, handsome MAID: en, they put a necklace of dried figs about my neck, and I was one of the Canephori.

LEADER OF CHORUS OF WOMEN: So surely I am bound to give my best advice to Athens. What matters that I was born a woman, if I can cure your misfortunes? I pay my share of tolls and taxes, by giving men to the State. But you, you miserable greybeards, you contribute nothing to the public charges; on the contrary, you have wasted the treasure of our forefathers, as it was called, the treasure amassed in the days of the Persian Wars. You pay nothing at all in return; and into the bargain you endanger our lives and liberties by your mistakes. Have you one word to say for yourselves?... Ah! don't irritate me, you there, or I'll lay my slipper across your jaws; and it's pretty heavy.

CHORUS OF OLD MEN (singing): Outrage upon outrage! things are going from bad to worse. Let us punish the minxes, every one of us that has balls to boast of. Come, off with our tunics, for a man must savour of manhood; come, my friends, let us strip naked from head to foot. Courage, I say, we who in our day garrisoned Lipsydrion; let us be young again, and shake off eld.

LEADER OF CHORUS OF OLD MEN: If we give them the least hold over us, that's the end! their audacity will know no bounds! We shall see them building ships, and fighting sea-fights, like Artemisia; and, if they want to mount and ride as cavalry, we had best cashier the knights, for indeed women excel in riding, and have a fine. firm seat for the gallop. Just think of all those squadrons of Amazons Micon has painted for us engaged in hand-to-hand combat with men. Come Then, we must now fit collars to all these willing necks.

CHORUS OF WOMEN (singing): By the blessed goddesses, if you anger me, I will let loose the beast of my evil passions, and a very hailstorm of blows will set you yelling for help. Come, dames, off with your tunics, and quick's the word; women must smell the smell of women in the throes of passion.... Now just you dare to measure strength with me, old greybeard, and I warrant you you'll never eat garlic or black beans any more. No, not a word! my anger is at boiling point, and I'll do with you what the beetle did with the eagle's eggs.

LEADER OF CHORUS OF WOMEN: I laugh at your threats, so long as I have on my side LAMPITO here, and the noble Theban, my dear Ismenia.... Pass decree on decree, you can do us no hurt, you wretch abhorred of all your fellows. Why, only yesterday, on occasion of the feast of Hecate, I asked my neighbours of Boeotia for one of their daughters for whom my girls have a lively liking -a fine, fat eel to wit; and if they did not refuse, all along of your silly decrees! We shall never cease to suffer the like, till someone gives you a neat trip-up and breaks your neck for you! (To LYSISTRATA: as she comes out from the Acropolis) You, Lysistrata, you who are leader of our glorious enterprise, why do I see you coming towards me with so gloomy an air?

LYSISTRATA: It's the behaviour of these naughty women, it's the female heart and female weakness that so discourage me.

LEADER OF CHORUS OF WOMEN: Tell us, tell us, what is it?

LYSISTRATA: I only tell the simple truth.

LEADER OF CHORUS OF WOMEN: What has happened so disconcerting? Come, tell your friends.

32

LYSISTRATA: Oh! the thing is so hard to tell-yet so impossible to conceal.

LEADER OF CHORUS OF WOMEN: Never seek to hide any ill that has befallen our cause.

LYSISTRATA: To blurt it out in a word-we want laying!

LEADER OF CHORUS OF WOMEN: Oh! Zeus, oh! Zeus!

LYSISTRATA: What use calling upon Zeus? The thing is even as I say. I cannot stop them any longer from lusting after the men. They are all for deserting. The first I caught was slipping out by the postern gate near the cave of Pan; another was letting herself down by a rope and pulley; a third was busy preparing her escape; while a fourth, perched on A BIRD: 's back, was just taking wing for Orsilochus' house, when I seized her by the hair. One and all, they are inventing excuses to be off home. (Pointing to the gate) Look! there goes one, trying to get out! Halloa there! whither away so fast?

FIRST WOMAN: I want to go home; I have some Milesian wool in the house, which is getting all eaten up by the worms.

LYSISTRATA: Bah! you and your worms! go back, I say!

FIRST WOMAN: I will return immediately, I swear I will by the two goddesses! I only have just to spread it out on the bed.

LYSISTRATA: You shall not do anything of the kind! I say, you shall not go.

FIRST WOMAN: Must I leave my wool to spoil then?

LYSISTRATA: Yes, if need be.

SECOND WOMAN: Unhappy woman that I am! Alas for my flax! I've left it at home unstript!

LYSISTRATA: So, here's another trying to escape to go home and strip her flax!

SECOND WOMAN: Oh! I swear by the goddess of light, the instant I have put it in condition I will come straight back.

LYSISTRATA: You shall do nothing of the kind! If once you began, others would want to follow suit.

THIRD WOMAN: Oh! goddess divine, Ilithyia, patroness of women in labour, stay, stay the birth, till I have reached a spot less hallowed than Athene's mount!

LYSISTRATA: What mean you by these silly tales?

THIRD WOMAN: I am going to have a child-now, this minute!

LYSISTRATA: But you were not pregnant yesterday!

THIRD WOMAN: Well, I am to-day. Oh! let me go in search of the midwife, Lysistrata, quick, quick!

LYSISTRATA: What is this fable you are telling me? (Feeling her stomach) Ah! what have you got there so hard?

THIRD WOMAN: A male child.

LYSISTRATA: No, no, by Aphrodite! nothing of the sort! Why, it feels like something hollow-a pot or a kettle. (Opening her robe) Oh! you silly creature, if you have not got the sacred helmet of Pallas-and you said you were with child!

THIRD WOMAN: And so I am, by Zeus, I am!

LYSISTRATA: Then why this helmet, pray?

THIRD WOMAN: For fear my pains should seize me in the Acropolis; I mean to lay my eggs in this helmet, as the doves do.

LYSISTRATA: Excuses and pretences every word! the thing's as clear as daylight. Anyway, you must stay here now till the fifth day, your day of purification.

THIRD WOMAN: I cannot sleep any more in the Acropolis, now I have seen the snake that guards the temple.

FOURTH WOMAN: Ah! and those awful owls with their dismal hooting! I cannot get a wink of rest, and I'm just dying of fatigue.

LYSISTRATA: You wicked women, have done with your falsehoods! You want your husbands, that's plain enough. But don't you think they want you just as badly? They are spending dreadful nights, oh! I know that well enough. But hold out, my dears, hold out! A little more patience, and the victory will be ours. An oracle promises us success, if only we remain united. Shall I repeat the words?

THIRD WOMAN: Yes, tell us what the oracle declares.

LYSISTRATA: Silence then! Now-"Whenas the swallows, fleeing before the hoopoes, shall have all flocked together in one place, and shall refrain them from all amorous commerce, then will be the end of all the ills of life; yea, and Zeus, who doth thunder in the skies, shall set above what was erst below...."

THIRD WOMAN: What! shall the men be underneath?

LYSISTRATA: "But if dissension do arise among the swallows, and they take wing from the holy temple, it will be said there is never a more wanton bird in all the world."

THIRD WOMAN: Ye gods! the prophecy is clear.

LYSISTRATA: Nay, never let us be cast down by calamity! Let us be brave to bear, and go back to our posts. It would be shameful indeed not to trust the promises of the oracle.

(They all go back into the Acropolis.)

CHORUS OF OLD MEN (singing): I want to tell you a fable they used to relate to me when I was a little boy. This is it: Once upon a time there was a young man called Melanion, who hated the thought of marriage so sorely that he fled away to the wilds. So he dwelt in the mountains, wove himself nets, and caught hares. He never, never came back, he had such a horror of women. As chaste as Melanion, we loathe the jades just as much as he did.

AN OLD MAN (beginning a brief duet with one of the women): You dear old woman, I would fain kiss you.

WOMAN: I will set you crying without onions.

OLD MAN: And give you a sound kicking.

WOMAN (pointing): Ah, ha! what a dense forest you have there!

OLD MAN: So was Myronides one of the bushiest of men of this side; his backside was all black, and he terrified his enemies as much as Phormio.

CHORUS OF WOMEN (singing): I want to tell you a fable too, to match yours about Melanion. Once there was a certain man called Timon, a tough customer, and a whimsical, a true son of the Furies, with a face that seemed to glare out of a thorn-bush. He withdrew from the world because he couldn't abide bad men, after vomiting a thousand curses at them. He had a holy horror of ill-conditioned fellows, but he was mighty tender towards women.

WOMAN (beginning another duet): Suppose I up and broke your jaw for you!

OLD MAN: I am not a bit afraid of you.

WOMAN: Suppose I let fly a good kick at you?

OLD MAN: I should see your thing then.

WOMAN: You would see that, for all my age, it is very well plucked.

LYSISTRATA (rushing out of the Acropolis): Ho there! come quick, come quick!

ONE OF THE WOMEN: What is it? Why these cries?

LYSISTRATA: A man! a man! I see him approaching all afire with the flames of love. Oh! divine Queen of Cyprus, Paphos and Cythera, I pray you still be propitious to our enterprise.

WOMAN: Where is he, this unknown foe?

LYSISTRATA: Over there-beside the Temple of Demeter.

WOMAN: Yes, indeed, I see him; but who is he?
LYSISTRATA: Look, look! do any of you recognize him?

MYRRHINE (joyfully): I do, I do! it's my husband Cinesias.

LYSISTRATA: To work then! Be it your task to inflame and torture and torment him. Seductions, caresses, provocations, refusals, try every means! Grant every favour,-always excepting what is forbidden by our oath on the wine-bowl.

MYRRHINE: Have no fear, I'll do it.

LYSISTRATA: Well, I shall stay here to help you cajole the man and set his passions aflame. The rest of you withdraw.

(CINESIAS: enters, in obvious and extreme sexual excitement. A slave follows him carrying an infant.)

CINESIAS: Alas! alas! how I am tortured by spasm and rigid convulsion! Oh! I am racked on the wheel!

LYSISTRATA: Who is this that dares to pass our lines?

CINESIAS: It is I.

LYSISTRATA: What, a man?

CINESIAS: Very much so!

LYSISTRATA: Get out.

CINESIAS: But who are you that thus repulses me?

LYSISTRATA: The sentinel of the day.

CINESIAS: For the gods' sake, call Myrrhine.

LYSISTRATA: Call Myrrhine, you say? And who are you?

CINESIAS: I am her husband, Cinesias, son of Paeon.

LYSISTRATA: Ah! good day, my dear friend. Your name is not unknown amongst us. Your wife has it forever on her lips; and she never touches an egg or an apple without saying: "This is for Cinesias."

CINESIAS: Really and truly?

LYSISTRATA: Yes, indeed, by Aphrodite! And if we fall to talking of men, quick your wife declares: "Oh! all the rest, they're good for nothing compared with Cinesias."

CINESIAS: Oh! please, please go and call her to me!

LYSISTRATA: And what will you give me for my trouble?

CINESIAS: Anything I've got, if you like. (Pointing to the evidence of his condition) I will give you what I have here!

LYSISTRATA: Well, well, I will tell her to come.

(She enters the Acropolis.)

CINESIAS: Quick, oh! be quick! Life has no more charms for me since she left my house. I am sad, sad, when I go indoors; it all seems so empty; my victuals have lost their savour. And all because of this erection that I can't get rid of!

MYRRHINE (to LYSISTRATA, over her shoulder): I love him, oh! I love him; but he won't let himself be loved. No! I shall not come.

CINESIAS: Myrrhine, my little darling Myrrhine, what are you saying? Come down to me quick.

MYRRHINE: No indeed, not I.

CINESIAS: I call you, Myrrhine, Myrrhine; won't you please come?

MYRRHINE: Why should you call me? You do not want me.

CINESIAS: Not want you! Why, here I stand, stiff with desire!

MYRRHINE: Good-bye.

(She turns, as if to go.)

CINESIAS: Oh! Myrrhine, Myrrhine, in our child's name, hear me; at any rate hear the child! Little lad, call your mother.

CHILD: Mamma, mamma, mamma!

CINESIAS: There, listen! Don't you pity the poor child? It's six days now you've never washed and never fed the child.

MYRRHINE: Poor darling, your father takes mighty little care of you!

CINESIAS: Come down, dearest, come down for the child's sake.

MYRRHINE: Ah! what a thing it is to be a mother! Well, well, we must come down, I suppose.

CINESIAS (as MYRRHINE: approaches): Why, how much younger and prettier she looks! And how she looks at me so lovingly! Her cruelty and scorn only redouble my passion.

MYRRHINE (ignoring him; to the child): You are as sweet as your father is provoking! Let me kiss you, my treasure, mother's darling!

CINESIAS: Ah! what a bad thing it is to let yourself be led away by other women! Why give me such pain and suffering, and yourself into the bargain?

MYRRHINE (as he is about to embrace her): Hands off, sir!

CINESIAS: Everything is going to rack and ruin in the house.

MYRRHINE: I don't care.

CINESIAS: But your web that's all being pecked to pieces by the cocks and hens, don't you care for that?

MYRRHINE: Precious little.

CINESIAS: And Aphrodite, whose mysteries you have not celebrated for so long? Oh! won't you please come back home?

MYRRHINE: No, least, not till a sound treaty puts an end to the war.

CINESIAS: Well, if you wish it so much, why, we'll make it, your treaty.

MYRRHINE: Well and good! When that's done, I will come home. Till then, I am bound by an oath.

CINESIAS: At any rate, lie with me for a little while.

MYRRHINE: No, no, no! (she hesitates) but just the same I can't say I don't love you.

CINESIAS: You love me? Then why refuse to lie with me, my little girl, my sweet Myrrhine?

MYRRHINE (pretending to be shocked): You must be joking! What, before the child!

CINESIAS (to the slave): Manes, carry the lad home. There, you see, the child is gone; there's nothing to hinder us; won't you lie down now?

MYRRHINE: But, miserable man, where, where?

CINESIAS: In the cave of Pan; nothing could be better.

MYRRHINE: But how shall I purify myself before going back into the citadel?

CINESIAS: Nothing easier! you can wash at the Clepsydra.

MYRRHINE: But my oath? Do you want me to perjure myself?

CINESIAS: I'll take all responsibility; don't worry.

MYRRHINE: Well, I'll be off, then, and find a bed for us.

CINESIAS: There's no point in that; surely we can lie on the ground.

MYRRHINE: No, no! even though you are bad, I don't like your lying on the bare earth.

(She goes back into the Acropolis.)

CINESIAS (enraptured): Ah! how the dear girl loves me!

41

MYRRHINE (coming back with a cot): Come, get to bed quick; I am going to undress. But, oh dear, we must get a mattress.

CINESIAS: A mattress? Oh! no, never mind about that!

MYRRHINE: No, by Artemis! lie on the bare sacking? never! That would be squalid.

CINESIAS: Kiss me!

MYRRHINE: Wait a minute!

(She leaves him again.)

CINESIAS: Good god, hurry up

MYRRHINE (coming back with a mattress): Here is a mattress. Lie down, I am just going to undress. But you've got no pillow.

CINESIAS: I don't want one either!

MYRRHINE: But I do.

(She leaves him again.)

CINESIAS: Oh god, oh god, she treats my tool just like HERACLES: !

MYRRHINE (coming back with a pillow): There, lift your head, dear! (Wondering what else to tantalize him with; to herself) Is that all, I wonder?

CINESIAS (misunderstanding): Surely. there's nothing else. Come, my treasure.

MYRRHINE: I am just unfastening my girdle. But remember what you promised me about making peace; mind you keep your word.

CINESIAS: Yes, yes, upon my life I will.

MYRRHINE: Why, you have no blanket!

CINESIAS: My god, what difference does that make? What I want is to make love!

MYRRHINE (going out again): Never fear-directly, directly! I'll be back in no time.

CINESIAS: The woman will kill me with her blankets!

MYRRHINE (coming back with a blanket): Now, get yourself up.

CINESIAS (pointing): I've got this up!

MYRRHINE: Wouldn't you like me to scent you?

CINESIAS: No, by Apollo, no, please don't!

MYRRHINE: Yes, by Aphrodite, but I will, whether you like it or not. (She goes out again.)

CINESIAS: God, I wish she'd hurry up and get through with all this!

MYRRHINE (coming back with a flask of perfume): Hold out your hand; now rub it in.

CINESIAS: Oh! in Apollo's name, I don't much like the smell of it; but perhaps it will improve when it's well rubbed in. It does not somehow smack of the marriage bed!

MYRRHINE: Oh dear! what a scatterbrain I am; if I haven't gone and brought Rhodian perfumes!

CINESIAS: Never mind, dearest, let it go now.

43

MYRRHINE: You don't really mean that.

(She goes.)

CINESIAS: Damn the man who invented perfumes!

MYRRHINE (coming back with another flask): Here, take this bottle.

CINESIAS: I have a better one all ready for you, darling. Come, you provoking creature, to bed with you, and don't bring another thing.

MYRRHINE: Coming, coming; I'm just slipping off my shoes. Dear boy, will you vote for peace?

CINESIAS: I'll think about it. (MYRRHINE: runs away.) I'm a dead man, she is killing me! She has gone, and left me in torment! (in tragic style) I must have someone to lay, I must! Ah me! the loveliest of women has choused and cheated me. Poor little lad, how am I to give you what you want so badly? Where is Cynalopex? quick, man, get him a nurse, do!

LEADER OF CHORUS OF OLD MEN: Poor, miserable wretch, baulked in your amorousness! what tortures are yours! Ah! you fill me with pity. Could any man's back and loins stand such a strain. He stands stiff and rigid, and there's never a wench to help him!

CINESIAS: Ye gods in heaven, what pains I suffer!

LEADER OF CHORUS OF OLD MEN: Well, there it is; it's her doing, that abandoned hussy!

CINESIAS: No, no! rather say that sweetest, dearest darling.

(He departs.)

LEADER OF CHORUS OF OLD MEN: That dearest darling? no, no, that hussy, say I! Zeus, thou god of the skies, canst not let loose a hurricane, to sweep them all up into the air, and whirl them round, then drop them down crash! and impale them on the point of this man's tool!

(A Spartan HERALD enters; he shows signs of being in the same condition as CINESIAS.)

HERALD: : Say, where shall I find the Senate and the Prytanes? I am bearer of dIspatches.

(An Athenian MAGISTRATE enters.)

MAGISTRATE: Are you a man or a Priapus?

HERALD: (with an effort at officiousness): Don't be stupid! I am a HERALD, of course, I swear I am, and I come from Sparta about making peace.

MAGISTRATE (pointing): But look, you are hiding a lance under your clothes, surely.

HERALD: : (embarrassed): No, nothing of the sort.

MAGISTRATE: Then why do you turn away like that, and hold your cloak out from your body? Have you got swellings in the groin from your journey?

HERALD: : By the twin brethren! the man's an old maniac.

MAGISTRATE: But you've got an erection! You lewd fellow!

HERALD: : I tell you no! but enough of this foolery.

MAGISTRATE (pointing): Well, what is it you have there then?

HERALD: : A Lacedaemonian 'skytale.'

MAGISTRATE: Oh, indeed, a 'skytale,' is it? Well, well, speak out frankly; I know all about these matters. How are things going at Sparta now?

HERALD: : Why, everything is turned upside down at Sparta; and all the allies have erections. We simply must have Pellene.

MAGISTRATE: What is the reason of it all? Is it the god Pan's doing?

HERALD: : No, it's all the work of LAMPITO: and the women who are acting at her instigation; they have kicked the men out from between their thighs.

MAGISTRATE: But what are you doing about it?

HERALD: We are at our wits' end; we walk bent double, just as if we were carrying lanterns in a wind. The jades have sworn we shall not so much as touch them till we have all agreed to conclude peace.

MAGISTRATE: Ah! I see now, it's a general conspiracy embracing all Greece. Go back to Sparta and bid them send envoys plenipotentiary to treat for peace. I will urge our Senators myself to name plenipotentiaries from us; and to persuade them, why, I will show them my own tool.

HERALD: : What could be better? I fly at your command.

(They go out in opposite directions.)

LEADER OF CHORUS OF OLD MEN: No wild beast is there, no flame of fire, more fierce and untamable than woman; the leopard is less savage and shameless.

LEADER OF CHORUS OF WOMEN: And yet you dare to make war upon me, wretch, when you might have me for your most faithful friend and ally.

LEADER OF CHORUS OF OLD MEN: Never, never can my hatred cease towards women.

LEADER OF CHORUS OF WOMEN: Well, suit yourself. Still I cannot bear to leave you all naked as you are; folks would laugh at you. Come, I am going to put this tunic on you.

LEADER OF CHORUS OF OLD MEN: You are right, upon my word! it was only in my confounded fit of rage that I took it off.

LEADER OF CHORUS OF WOMEN: Now at any rate you look like a man, and they won't make fun of you. Ah! if you had not offended me so badly, I would take out that nasty insect you have in your eye for you.

LEADER OF CHORUS OF OLD MEN: Ah! so that's what was annoying me so Look, here's a ring, just remove the insect, and show it to me. By Zeus! it has been hurting my eye for a long time now.

LEADER OF CHORUS OF WOMEN: Well, I agree, though your manners are not over and above pleasant. Oh I what a huge great gnat! just look! It's from Tricorythus, for sure.

LEADER OF CHORUS OF OLD MEN: A thousand thanks! the creature was digging a regular well in my eye; now that it's gone, my tears can flow freely.

LEADER OF CHORUS OF WOMEN: I will wipe them for you-bad, naughty man though you are. Now, just one kiss.

LEADER OF CHORUS OF OLD MEN: A kiss? certainly not.

LEADER OF CHORUS OF WOMEN: Just one, whether you like it or not.

LEADER OF CHORUS OF OLD MEN: Oh! those confounded women! how they do cajole us! How true the saying: "'Tis impossible to live with the baggages, impossible to live without 'em!" Come, let us agree for the future not to regard each other anymore as enemies; and to clinch the bargain, let us sing a choric song.

COMBINED CHORUS OF WOMEN AND OLD MEN (singing): We desire, Athenians, to speak ill of no man; but on the contrary to say much good of everyone, and to do the like. We have had enough of misfortunes and calamities. If there is any man or woman who wants a bit of money-two or three minas or so; well, our purse is full. If only peace is concluded, the borrower will not have to pay back. Also I'm inviting to supper a few Carystian friends, who are excellently well qualified. I have still a drop of good soup left, and a young porker I'm going to kill, and the flesh will be sweet and tender. I shall expect you at my house to-day; but first away to the baths with you, you and your children; then come all of you, ask no one's leave, but walk straight up, as if you were at home; never fear, the door will be... shut in your faces!

LEADER OF CHORUS OF OLD MEN: Ah! here come the envoys from Sparta with their long flowing beards; why, you would think they wore pigstyes between their thighs.

(Enter the LACONIAN ENVOYS afflicted like their HERALD.) Hail to you, first of all, Laconians; then tell us how you fare.

LACONIAN ENVOY: No need for many words; you can see what a state we are in.

LEADER OF CHORUS OF OLD MEN: Alas! the situation grows more and more strained! the intensity of the thing is simply frightful.

LACONIAN ENVOY: It's beyond belief. But to work! summon your Commissioners, and let us patch up the best peace we may.

LEADER OF CHORUS OF OLD MEN: Ah! our men too, like wrestlers in the arena, cannot endure a rag over their bellies; it's an athlete's malady, which only exercise can remedy.

(The MAGISTRATE: returns; he too now has an evident reason to desire peace.)

MAGISTRATE: Can anybody tell us where LYSISTRATA: is? Surely she will have some compassion on our condition.

LEADER OF CHORUS OF OLD MEN (pointing): Look! now he has the very same complaint. (To the MAGISTRATE) Don't you feel a strong nervous tension in the morning?

MAGISTRATE: Yes, and a dreadful, dreadful torture it is! Unless peace is made very soon, we shall find no recourse but to make love to Clisthenes.

LEADER OF CHORUS OF OLD MEN: Take my advice, and arrange your clothes as best you can; one of the fellows who mutilated the Hermae might see you.

MAGISTRATE: Right, by Zeus.

(He endeavours, not too successfully, to conceal his condition.)

LACONIAN ENVOY: Quite right, by the Dioscuri. There, I will put on my tunic.

MAGISTRATE: Oh! what a terrible state we are in! Greeting to you, Laconian fellow-sufferers.

LACONIAN ENVOY (addressing one of his countrymen): Ah! my boy, what a terrible thing it would have been if these fellows had seen us just now when we were on full stand!

MAGISTRATE: Speak out, Laconians, what is it brings you here?

LACONIAN ENVOY: We have come to treat for peace.

MAGISTRATE: Well said; we are of the same mind. Better call Lysistrata, then; she is the only person will bring us to terms.

LACONIAN ENVOY: Yes, yes-and Lysistratus into the bargain, if you will.

MAGISTRATE: Needless to call her; she has heard your voices, and here she comes.

(She comes out of the Acropolis.)

LEADER OF CHORUS OF OLD MEN: Hail, boldest and bravest of womankind! The time is come to show yourself in turn uncompromising and conciliatory, exacting and yielding, haughty and condescending. Call up all your skill and artfulness. Lo! the foremost men in Hellas, seduced by your fascinations, are agreed to entrust you with the task of ending their quarrels.

LYSISTRATA: It will be an easy task-if only they refrain from mutual indulgence in masculine love; if they do, I shall know the fact at once. Now, where is the gentle goddess Peace? (The goddess, in the form of a beautiful nude girl is brought in by the Machine.) Lead hither the Laconian envoys. But, look you, no roughness or violence; our husbands always behaved so boorishly. Bring them to me with smiles, as women should. If any refuse to give you his hand, then take hold of his tool. Bring up the Athenians too; you may lead them either way. Laconians, approach; and you, Athenians, on my other side. Now hearken all! I am but a woman; but I have good common sense; Nature has endowed me with discriminating judgment, which I have yet further developed, thanks to the wise teachings of my father and the elders of the city. First I must bring a reproach against you that applies equally to both sides. At Olympia, and Thermopylae, and Delphi, and a score of other places too numerous to mention, you celebrate before the same altars ceremonies common to all Hellenes; yet you go cutting each other's throats, and sacking Hellenic cities, when all the while the barbarian yonder is threatening you! That is my first point.

MAGISTRATE (devouring the goddess with his eyes): Good god, this erection is killing me!

LYSISTRATA: Now it is to you I address myself, Laconians. Have you forgotten how Periclidas, your own countryman, sat a suppliant before our altars? How pale he was in his purple robes! He had come to crave an army of us; it was the time when Messenia was pressing you sore, and the Sea-god was shaking the earth. Cimon marched to your aid at the head of four thousand hoplites, and saved Lacedaemon. And, after such a service as that, you ravage the soil of your benefactors!

50

MAGISTRATE: They do wrong, very wrong, Lysistrata.

LACONIAN ENVOY: We do wrong, very wrong. (Looking at the goddess) Ah! great gods! what a lovely bottom Peace has!

LYSISTRATA: And now a word to the Athenians. Have you no memory left of how, in the days when you wore the tunic of slaves, the Laconians came, spear in hand, and slew a host of Thessalians and partisans of Hippias the tyrant? They, and they only, fought on your side on that eventful day; they delivered you from despotism, and thanks to them our nation could change the short tunic of the slave for the long cloak of the free man.

LACONIAN ENVOY (looking at LYSISTRATA): I have never see a woman of more gracious dignity.

MAGISTRATE (looking at PEACE): I have never seen a woman with a finer body!

LYSISTRATA: Bound by such ties of mutual kindness, how can you bear to be at war? Stop, stay the hateful strife, be reconciled; what hinders you?

LACONIAN ENVOY: We are quite ready, if they will give us back our rampart.

LYSISTRATA: What rampart, my dear man?

LACONIAN ENVOY: Pylos, which we have been asking for and craving for ever so long.

MAGISTRATE: In the Sea-god's name, you shall never have it!

LYSISTRATA: Agree, my friends, agree.

MAGISTRATE: But then what city shall we be able to stir up trouble in?

LYSISTRATA: Ask for another place in exchange.

MAGISTRATE: Ah! that's the ticket! Well, to begin with, give us Echinus, the Maliac gulf adjoining, and the two legs of Megara.

LACONIAN ENVOY: No, by the Dioscuri, surely not all that, my dear sir.

LYSISTRATA: Come to terms; never make a difficulty of two legs more or less!

MAGISTRATE (his eye on PEACE): Well, I'm ready to strip down and get to work right now.

(He takes off his mantle.)
LACONIAN ENVOY (following out this idea): And I also, to dung it to start with.

LYSISTRATA: That's just what you shall do, once peace is signed. So, if you really want to make it, go consult your allies about the matter.

MAGISTRATE: What allies, I should like to know? Why, we are all erected; there's no one who is not mad to be mating. What we all want is to be in bed with our wives; how should our allies fail to second our project?

LACONIAN ENVOY: And ours too, for certain sure!

MAGISTRATE: The Carystians first and foremost by the gods!

LYSISTRATA: Well said, indeed! Now go and purify yourselves for entering the Acropolis, where the women invite you to supper; we will empty our provision baskets to do you honour. At table, you will exchange oaths and pledges; then each man will go home with his wife.

MAGISTRATE: Come along then, and as quick as may be.

LACONIAN ENVOY: Lead on; I'm your man.

MAGISTRATE: Quick, quick's the word, say I.

(They follow LYSISTRATA: into the Acropolis.)

CHORUS OF WOMEN (singing): Embroidered stuffs, and dainty tunics, and flowing gowns, and golden ornaments, everything I have, I offer them to you with all my heart; take them all for your children, for your girls, in case they are chosen Canephori. I invite you every one to enter, come in and choose whatever you will; there is nothing so well fastened, you cannot break the seals, and carry away the contents. Look about you everywhere. . . you won't find a blessed thing, unless you have sharper eyes than mine. And if any of you lacks corn to feed his slaves and his young and numerous family, why, I have a few grains of wheat at home; let him take what I have to give, a big twelve-pound loaf included. So let my poorer neighbours all come with bags and wallets; my man, Manes, shall give them corn; but I warn them not to come near my door, but-beware the dog!

(Another MAGISTRATE: enters, and begins knocking at the gate.)

SECOND MAGISTRATE: I say, you, open the door! (To the WOMEN) Go your way, I tell you. (As the women sit down in front of the gate) Why, bless me, they're sitting down now; I shall have to singe 'em with my torch to make 'em stir! What impudence! I won't take this. Oh, well, if it's absolutely necessary, just to please you, we'll have to take the trouble.

AN ATHENIAN: And I'll share it with you.

(He brandishes the torch he is carrying and the CHORUS OF WOMEN departs. The CHORUS OF OLD MEN: follows shortly after.)

SECOND MAGISTRATE: No, no, you must be off-or I'll tear your hair out, I will; be off, I say, and don't annoy the Laconian envoys; they're just coming out from the banquet-ball.

ATHENIAN: Such a merry banquet I've never seen before! The Laconians were simply charming. After the drink is in, why, we're all wise men, every one of us.

53

MAGISTRATE: It's only natural, to be sure, for sober, we're all fools. Take my advice, my fellow-countrymen, our envoys should always be drunk. We go to Sparta; we enter the city sober; why, we must be picking a quarrel directly. We don't understand what they say to us, we imagine a lot they don't say at all, and we report home all wrong, all topsy-urvy. But, look you, to-day it's quite Different; we're enchanted whatever happens; instead of Clitagora, they might sing us Telamon, and we should clap our hands just the same. A perjury or two into the bargain, why! What does that matter to merry companions in their cups? (The two CHORUSES return.) But here they are back again! Will you begone, you loafing scoundrels. (The CHORUSES retire again.)

ATHENIAN: Ah ha! here's the company coming out already.

(Two choruses, one Laconian and one Athenian, enter, dancing to the music of flutes; they are followed by the women under the leadership of LYSISTRATA.)

A LACONIAN: My dear, sweet friend, come, take your flute in hand; I would fain dance and sing my best in honour of the Athenians and our noble selves.

ATHENIAN: Yes, take your flute, in the gods'name. What a delight to see him dance!

LACONIAN (dancing and singing): Oh! Mnemosyne! inspire these men, inspire my muse who knows our exploits and those of the Athenians. With what a god-like ardour did they swoop down at Artemisium on the ships of the Medes! What a glorious victory was that! For the soldiers of Leonidas, they were like fierce boars whetting their tusks. The sweat ran down their faces, and drenched all their limbs, for verily the Persians were as many as the sands of the seashore. Oh! Artemis, huntress queen, whose arrows pierce the denizens of the woods, virgin goddess, be thou favourable to the peace we here conclude; through thee may our hearts be long united! May this treaty draw close for ever the bonds of a happy friendship! No more wiles and stratagems! Aid us, oh! aid us, MAID: en huntress!

MAGISTRATE: All is for the best; and now, Laconians, take your wives away home with you, and you, Athenians, yours. May husband live happily with wife, and wife with husband. Dance, dance, to celebrate our bliss, and let us be heedful to avoid like mistakes for the future.

CHORUS OF ATHENIANS (singing): Appear, appear, dancers, and the Graces with you! Let us invoke, one and all, Artemis, and her heavenly brother, gracious Apollo, patron of the dance, and DIONYSUS: , whose eye darts flame, as he steps forward surrounded by the Maenad MAID: s, and Zeus, who wields the flashing lightning, and his august, thrice-blessed spouse, the Queen of Heaven! These let us invoke, and all the other gods, calling all the inhabitants of the skies to witness the noble Peace now concluded under the fond auspices of Aphrodite. Io Paean! Io Paean! dance, leap, as in honour of a victory won. Euoi! Euoi! Euai! Euai!

MAGISTRATE: And you, our Laconian guests, sing us a new and inspiring strain!

LACONIAN (singing): Leave once more, oh! leave once more the noble height of Taygetus, oh! Muse of Lacedaemon, and join us in singing the praises of Apollo
of Amyclae, and Athene of the Brazen House, and the gallant twin sons of Tyndareus, who practise arms on the banks of the Eurotas river. Haste, haste hither with nimble-footed pace, let us sing Sparta, the city that delights in choruses divinely sweet and graceful dances, when our MAID: ens bound lightly by the river side, like frolicsome fillies, beating the ground with rapid steps and shaking their long locks in the wind, as Bacchantes wave their wands in the wild revels of the Wine-god. At their head, oh! chaste and beauteous goddess, daughter of Leto, Artemis, do thou lead the song and dance. With a fillet binding thy waving tresses, appear in thy loveliness; leap like a fawn, strike thy divine hands together to animate the dance, and aid us to renown the valiant goddess of battles, great Athene of the Brazen House!

(All depart, singing and dancing.)

THE END

THE CLOUDS

CHARACTERS

STREPSIADES

PHIDIPPIDES

SERVANT OF STREPSIADES

DISCIPLES OF SOCRATES

SOCRATES

JUST DISCOURSE

UNJUST DISCOURSE

PASIAS, a Money-lender

AMYNIAS, another Money-lender

CHORUS OF CLOUDS

The Play **SCENE**:-In the background are two houses, that of Strepsiades and that of Socrates: , the Thoughtery. The latter is small and dingy; the interior of the former is shown and two beds are seen, each occupied.)

STREPSIADES: (sitting up) GREAT gods! will these nights never end? will daylight never come? I heard the cock crow long ago and my slaves are snoring still! Ah! Ah! It wasn't like this formerly. Curses on the war! has it not done me ills enough? Now I may not even chastise my own slaves. Again there's this brave lad, who never wakes the whole long night, but, wrapped in his five coverlets, farts away to his heart's content. (He lies down) Come! let me nestle in well and snore too, if it be possible....oh! misery, it's vain to think of sleep with all these expenses, this stable, these debts, which are devouring me, thanks to this fine cavalier, who only knows how to look after his long locks, to show himself off in his chariot and to dream of horses! And I, I am nearly dead, when I see the moon bringing the third decade in her train and my liability falling due....Slave! light the lamp and bring me my tablets. (The slave obeys.) Who are all my creditors?   Let me see and reckon up the interest. What is it I owe?....Twelve   minae to Pasias....What! twelve minae to Pasias?....Why did I borrow these? Ah! I know! It was to buy that thoroughbred, which cost me so much. How I should have prized the stone that had blinded him!

PHIDIPPIDES: (in his sleep) That's not fair, Philo! Drive your chariot straight, I say.

STREPSIADES: This is what is destroying me. He raves about horses, even in his sleep.

PHIDIPPIDES: (still sleeping) How many times round the track is the race for the chariots of war?

STREPSIADES: It's your own father you are driving to death....to ruin. Come! what debt comes next, after that of Pasias?....Three minae to   Amynias for a chariot and its two wheels.

PHIDIPPIDES: (still asleep) Give the horse a good roll in the dust and lead him home.

57

STREPSIADES: Ah! wretched boy! it's my money that you are making roll. My   creditors have distrained on my goods, and here are others again,   who demand security for their interest.

PHIDIPPIDES: (awaking) What is the matter with you, father, that you groan and turn about the whole night through?

STREPSIADES: I have a bum-bailiff in the bedclothes biting me.

PHIDIPPIDES: For pity's sake, let me have a little sleep.

(He turns over.)

STREPSIADES: Very well, sleep on! but remember that all these debts will fall back on your shoulders. Oh! curses on the go-between who made me marry your mother! I lived so happily in the country, a commonplace, everyday life, but a good and easy one-had not a trouble, not a care, was rich in bees, in sheep and in olives. Then indeed I had to marry the niece of Megacles, the son of Megacles; I belonged to the country, she was from the town; she was a haughty, extravagant woman, a true Coesyra. On the nuptial day, when I lay beside her, I was reeking of the dregs of the wine-cup, of cheese and of wool; she was redolent with essences, saffron, voluptuous kisses, the love of spending, of good cheer and of wanton delights. I will not say she did nothing; no, she worked hard...to ruin me, and pretending all the while merely to be showing her the cloak she had woven for me, I said, "Wife you go too fast about your work, your threads are too closely woven and you use far too much wool." (A slave enters witk a lamp.)

SLAVE: There is no more oil in the lamp.

STREPSIADES: Why then did you light such a thirsty lamp? Come here, I am going to beat you.

SLAVE: What for?

STREPSIADES: Because you have put in too thick a wick....Later, when we had this boy, what was to be his name? It was the cause of much quarrelling with my loving wife. She insisted on having some reference to a horse in his name, that he should be called Xanthippus, Charippus or Callippides. I wanted to name him Phidonides after his grandfather. We disputed long, and finally agreed to style him

PHIDIPPIDES: ....She used to fondle and coax him, saying, "Oh! what a joy it will be to me when you have grown up, to see you, like my father, Megacles, clothed in purple and standing up straight in your chariot driving your steeds toward the town." And I would say to him, "When, like your father, you will go, dressed in a skin, to fetch back your goats from Phelleus." Alas! he never listened to me and his madness for horses has shattered my fortune. (He gets out of bed.) But by dint of thinking the livelong night, I have discovered a road to salvation, both miraculous and divine. If he will but follow it, I shall be out of my trouble! First, however, he must be awakened, but it must be done as gently as possible. How shall I manage it? Phidippides! my little Phidippides!

PHIDIPPIDES: (awaking again) What is it, father?

STREPSIADES: Kiss me and give me your hand.

PHIDIPPIDES: (getting up and doing as his father requests) There! What's it all about?

STREPSIADES: Tell me! do you love me?

PHIDIPPIDES: By Posidon, the equestrian Posidon! yes, I swear I do.

STREPSIADES: Oh, do not, I pray you, invoke this god of horses; he is the one who is the cause of all my cares. But if you really love me, and with your whole heart, my boy, believe me.

PHIDIPPIDES: Believe you? about what?

STREPSIADES: Alter your habits forthwith and go and learn what I tell you.

59

PHIDIPPIDES: Say on, what are your orders?

STREPSIADES: Will you obey me ever so little?

PHIDIPPIDES: By Bacchus, I will obey you.

STREPSIADES: Very well then! Look this way. Do you see that little door and that little house?

PHIDIPPIDES: Yes, father. But what are you driving at?

STREPSIADES: That is the Thoughtery of wise souls. There they prove that we are coals enclosed on all sides under a vast snuffer, which is the sky. If well paid, these men also teach one how to gain law-suits, whether they be just or not.

PHIDIPPIDES: What do they call themselves?

STREPSIADES: I do not know exactly, but they are deep thinkers and most admirable people.

PHIDIPPIDES: Bah! the wretches! I know them; you mean those quacks with pale faces, those barefoot fellows, such as that miserable Socrates and Chaerephon?

STREPSIADES: Silence! say nothing foolish! If you desire your father not to die of hunger, join their company and let your horses go.

PHIDIPPIDES: No, by Bacchus! even though you gave me the pheasants that Leogoras raises.

STREPSIADES: Oh! my beloved son, I beseech you, go and follow their teachings.

PHIDIPPIDES: And what is it I should learn?

STREPSIADES: It seems they have two courses of reasoning, the true and the false, and that, thanks to the false, the worst law-suits can be gained. If then you learn this science, which is false, I shall not have to pay an obolus of all the debts I have contracted on your account.

PHIDIPPIDES: No, I will not do it. I should no longer dare to look at our gallant horsemen, when I had so ruined my tan.

STREPSIADES: Well then, by Demeter! I will no longer support you, neither you, nor your team, nor your saddle-horse. Go and hang yourself, I turn you out of house and home.

PHIDIPPIDES: My uncle Megacles will not leave me without horses; I shall go to him and laugh at your anger. (He departs. Strepsiades goes over to Socrates' house.)

STREPSIADES: One rebuff shall not dishearten me. With the help of the gods I will enter the Thoughtery and learn myself. (He hesitates.) But at my age, memory has gone and the mind is slow to grasp things. How can all these fine distinctions, these subtleties be learned? (Making up his mind) Bah! why should I dally thus instead of rapping at the door? Slave, slave! (He knocks and calls.)

A DISCIPLE (from within) A plague on you! Who are you?

STREPSIADES: the son of Phido, of the deme of Cicynna.

DISCIPLE: (coming out of the door) You are nothing but an ignorant and illiterate fellow to let fly at the door with such kicks. You have brought on a miscarriage-of an idea!

STREPSIADES: Pardon me, please; for I live far away from here in the country. But tell me, what was the idea that miscarried?

DISCIPLE: I may not tell it to any but a disciple.

STREPSIADES: Then tell me without fear, for I have come to study among you.

DISCIPLE: Very well then, but reflect, that these are mysteries. Lately, a flea bit Chaerephon on the brow and then from there sprang on to the head of Socrates: Socrates: asked Chaerephon, "How many times the length of its legs does a flea jump?"

STREPSIADES: And how ever did he go about measuring it?

DISCIPLE: Oh! it was most ingenious! He melted some wax, seized the flea and dipped its two feet in the wax, which, when cooled, left them shod with true Persian slippers. These he took off and with them measured the distance.

STREPSIADES: Ah! great Zeus! what a brain! what subtlety!

DISCIPLE: I wonder what then would you say, if you knew another of Socrates' contrivances?

STREPSIADES: What is it? Pray tell me.

DISCIPLE: Chaerephon of the deme of Sphettia asked him whether he thought a gnat buzzed through its proboscis or through its anus.

STREPSIADES: And what did he say about the gnat?

DISCIPLE: He said that the gut of the gnat was narrow, and that, in passing through this tiny passage, the air is driven with force towards the breech; then after this slender channel, it encountered the rump, which was distended like a trumpet, and there it resounded sonorously.

STREPSIADES: So the arse of a gnat is a trumpet. Oh! what a splendid arsevation! Thrice happy Socrates ! It would not be difficult to succeed in a law-suit, knowing so much about a gnat's guts!

DISCIPLE: Not long ago a lizard caused him the loss of a sublime thought.

STREPSIADES: In what way, please?

DISCIPLE: One night, when he was studying the course of the moon and its revolutions and was gazing open-mouthed at the heavens, a lizard crapped upon him from the top of the roof.

STREPSIADES: A lizard crapping on Socrates! That's rich!

DISCIPLE: Last night we had nothing to eat.

STREPSIADES: Well, what did he contrive, to secure you some supper?

DISCIPLE: He spread over the table a light layer of cinders, bending an iron rod the while; then he took up a pair of compasses and at the same moment unhooked a piece of the victim which was hanging in the palaestra.

STREPSIADES: And we still dare to admire Thales! Open, open this home of knowledge to me quickly! Haste, haste to show me Socrates; I long to become his disciple. But do please open the door.

(The door opens, revealing the interior of the Thoughtery, in which the Disciples of Socrates are seen in various postures of meditation and study; they are pale and emaciated creatures.)

Ah! by HERACLES: What country are those animals from?

DISCIPLE: Why, what are you astonished at? What do you think they resemble?

STREPSIADES: The captives of Pylos. But why do they look so fixedly on the ground?

DISCIPLE: They are seeking for what is below the ground.

STREPSIADES: Ah! they're looking for onions. Do not give yourselves so much trouble; I know where there are some, fine
big ones. But what are those fellows doing, bent all double?

DISCIPLE: They are sounding the abysses of Tartarus.

STREPSIADES: And what are their arses looking at in the heavens?

DISCIPLE: They are studying astronomy on their own account. But come in so that the master may not find us here.

STREPSIADES: Not yet; not yet; let them not change their position. I want to tell them my own little matter.

DISCIPLE: But they may not stay too long in the open air and away from school.

STREPSIADES: (pointing to a celestial globe) In the name of all the gods, what is that? Tell me.

DISCIPLE: That is astronomy.

STREPSIADES: (pointing to a map) And that?

DISCIPLE: Geometry.

STREPSIADES: What is that used for?

DISCIPLE: To measure the land.

STREPSIADES: But that is apportioned by lot.

DISCIPLE: No, no, I mean the entire earth.

STREPSIADES: Ah! what a funny thing! How generally useful indeed is this invention!

DISCIPLE: There is the whole surface of the earth. Look! Here is Athens.

STREPSIADES: Athens! you are mistaken; I see no courts in session.

DISCIPLE: Nevertheless it is really and truly the Attic territory.

STREPSIADES: And where are my neighbours of Cicynna?

DISCIPLE They live here. This is Euboea; you see this island, that is so long and narrow.

STREPSIADES: I know. Because we and Pericles have stretched it by dint of squeezing it. And where is Lacedaemon?

DISCIPLE: Lacedaemon? Why, here it is, look.

STREPSIADES: How near it is to us! Think it well over, it must be removed to a greater distance.

DISCIPLE: But, by Zeus, that is not possible.

STREPSIADES: Then, woe to you! and who is this man suspended up in a basket?

DISCIPLE: That's himself.

STREPSIADES: Who's himself?

SOCRATES: ! Oh! I pray you, call him right loudly for me.

DISCIPLE: Call him yourself; I have no time to waste. (He departs. The machine swings in Socrates in a basket.)

STREPSIADES: Socrates: ! my little Socrates: !

SOCRATES: (loftily) Mortal, what do you want with me?

STREPSIADES: First, what are you doing up there? Tell me, I beseech you.

SOCRATES: (POMPOUSLY) I am traversing the air and contemplating the sun.

STREPSIADES: Thus it's not on the solid ground, but from the height of this basket, that you slight the gods, if indeed....

SOCRATES: I have to suspend my brain and mingle the subtle essence of my mind with this air, which is of the like nature, in order clearly to penetrate the things of heaven. I should have discovered nothing, had I remained on the ground to consider from below the things that are above; for the earth by its force attracts the sap of the mind to itself. It's just the same with the watercress.

STREPSIADES: What? Does the mind attract the sap of the watercress? Ah! my dear little Socrates, come down to me! I have come to ask you for lessons.

SOCRATES: (descending) And for what lessons?

STREPSIADES: I want to learn how to speak. I have borrowed money, and my merciles creditors do not leave me a moment's peace; all my goods are at stake.

SOCRATES: And how was it you did not see that you were getting so much into debt?

STREPSIADES: My ruin has been the madness for horses, a most rapacious evil; but teach me one of your two methods of reasoning, the one whose object is not to repay anything, and, may the gods bear witness, that I am ready to pay any fee you may name.

SOCRATES: By which gods will you swear? To begin with, the gods are not a coin current with us.

66

STREPSIADES: But what do you swear by then? By the iron money of Byzantium?

SOCRATES: Do you really wish to know the truth of celestial matters?

STREPSIADES: Why, yes, if it's possible.

SOCRATES: ....and to converse with the clouds, who are our genii?

STREPSIADES: Without a doubt.

SOCRATES: Then be seated on this sacred couch.

STREPSIADES: (sitting down) I am seated.

SOCRATES: Now take this chaplet.

STREPSIADES: Why a chaplet? Alas! Socrates, would you sacrifice me, like Athamas?

SOCRATES: No, these are the rites of initiation.

STREPSIADES: And what is it I am to gain?

SOCRATES: You will become a thorough rattle-pate, a hardened old stager, the fine flour of the talkers....But come, keep quiet.

STREPSIADES: By Zeus! That's no lie! Soon I shall be nothing but wheat-flour, if you powder me in that fashion.

SOCRATES: Silence, old man, give heed to the prayers. (In an hierophantic tone) Oh! most mighty king, the boundless air, that keepest the earth suspended in space, thou bright Aether and ye venerable goddesses, the Clouds, who carry in your loins the thunder and the lightning, arise, ye sovereign powers and manifest yourselves in the celestial spheres to the eyes of your sage.

67

STREPSIADES: Not yet! Wait a bit, till I fold my mantle double, so as not to get wet. And to think that I did not even bring my travelling cap! What a misfortune!

SOCRATES: (ignoring this) Come, oh! Clouds, whom I adore, come and show yourselves to this man, whether you be resting on the sacred summits of Olympus, crowned with hoar-frost, or tarrying in the gardens of Ocean, your father, forming sacred choruses with the Nymphs; whether you be gathering the waves of the Nile in golden vases or dwelling in the Maeotic marsh or on the snowy rocks of Mimas, hearken to my prayer and accept my offering. May these sacrifices be pleasing to you. (Amidst rumblings of thunder the CHORUS OF CLOUDS: : appears.)

CHORUS: (singing) Eternal Clouds, let us appear; let us arise from the roaring depths of Ocean, our father; let us fly towards the lofty mountains, spread our damp wings over their forest-laden summits, whence we will dominate the distant valleys, the harvest fed by the sacred earth, the murmur of the divine streams and the resounding waves of the sea, which the unwearying orb lights up with its glittering beams. But let us shake off the rainy fogs, which hide our immortal beauty and sweep the earth from afar with our gaze.

SOCRATES: Oh, venerated goddesses, yes, you are answering my call! (To Strepsiades .) Did you hear their voices mingling with the awful growling of the thunder?

STREPSIADES: Oh! adorable Clouds, I revere you and I too am going to let off my thunder, so greatly has your own affrighted me. (He farts.) Faith! Whether permitted or not, I must, I must crap!

SOCRATES: No scoffing; do not copy those damned comic poets. Come, silence! a numerous host of goddesses approaches with songs.

CHORUS: (singing) Virgins, who pour forth the rains, let us move toward Attica, the rich country of Pallas, the home of the brave; let us visit the dear land of Cecrops, where the secret rites are celebrated, where the mysterious sanctuary flies open to the initiate.... What victims are offered there to the deities of heaven! What glorious temples! What statues! What holy prayers to the rulers of Olympus! At every season nothing but sacred festivals, garlanded victims, is to be seen. Then Spring brings round again the joyous feasts of DIONYSUS: , the harmonious contests of the choruses and the serious melodies of the flute.

STREPSIADES: By Zeus! Tell me, Socrates, I pray you, who are these women, whose language is so solemn; can they be demi-goddesses?

SOCRATES: Not at all. They are the Clouds of heaven, great goddesses for the lazy; to them we owe all, thoughts, speeches, trickery, roguery, boasting, lies, sagacity.

STREPSIADES: Ah! that was why, as I listened to them, my mind spread out its wings; it burns to babble about trifles, to maintain worthless arguments, to voice its petty reasons, to contradict, to tease some opponent. But are they not going to show themselves? I should like to see them, were it possible.

SOCRATES: Well, look this way in the direction of Parnes; I already see those who are slowly descending.

STREPSIADES: But where, where? Show them to me.

SOCRATES: They are advancing in a throng, following an oblique path across the dales and thickets.

STREPSIADES: Strange! I can see nothing.

SOCRATES: There, close to the entrance.

STREPSIADES: Hardly, if at all, can I distinguish them.

SOCRATES: You must see them clearly now, unless your eyes are filled with gum as thick as pumpkins.

STREPSIADES: Aye, undoubtedly! Oh! the venerable goddesses! Why, they fill up the entire stage.

SOCRATES: And you did not know, you never suspected, that they were goddesses?

STREPSIADES: No, indeed; I thought the Clouds were only fog, dew and vapour.

SOCRATES: But what you certainly do not know is that they are the support of a crowd of quacks, the diviners, who were sent to Thurium, the notorious physicians, the well-combed fops, who load their fingers with rings down to the nails, and the braggarts, who write dithyrambic verses, all these are idlers whom the Clouds provide a living for, because they sing them in their verses.

STREPSIADES: It is then for this that they praise "the rapid flight of the moist clouds, which veil the brightness of day" and "the waving locks of the hundred-headed Typho" and "the impetuous tempests, which float through the heavens, like birds of prey with aerial wings loaded with mists" and "the rains, the dew, which the clouds outpour." As a reward for these fine phrases they bolt well-grown, tasty mullet and delicate thrushes.

SOCRATES: Yes, thanks to these. And is it not right and meet?

STREPSIADES: Tell me then why, if these really are the Clouds, they so very much resemble mortals. This is not their usual form.

SOCRATES: What are they like then?

STREPSIADES: I don't know exactly; well, they are like great packs of wool, but not like women-no, not in the least....And these have noses.

SOCRATES: Answer my questions.

STREPSIADES: Willingly! Go on, I am listening.

SOCRATES: Have you not sometimes seen clouds in the sky like a centaur, a leopard, a wolf or a bull?

STREPSIADES: Why, certainly I have, but what of that?

SOCRATES: They take what metamorphosis they like. If they see a debauchee with long flowing locks and hairy as a beast, like the son of Xenophantes, they take the form of a Centaur in derision of his shameful passion.

STREPSIADES: And when they see Simon, that thiever of public money, what do they do then?

SOCRATES: To picture him to the life, they turn at once into wolves.

STREPSIADES: So that was why yesterday, when they saw Cleonymus, who cast away his buckler because he is the veriest poltroon amongst men, they changed into deer.

SOCRATES: And to-day they have seen Clisthenes; you see....they are women Strepsiades Hail, sovereign goddesses, and if ever you have let your celestial voice be heard by mortal ears, speak to me, oh! speak to me, ye all-powerful queens.

CHORUS-LEADER: Hail! veteran of the ancient times, you who burn to instruct yourself in fine language. And you, great high-PRIEST: of subtle nonsense, tell us; your desire. To you and Prodicus alone of all the hollow orationers of to-day have we lent an ear-to Prodicus, because of his knowledge and his great wisdom, and to you, because you walk with head erect, a confident look, barefooted, resigned to everything and proud of our protection.

STREPSIADES: Oh! Earth! What august utterances! how sacred! how wondrous!

SOCRATES: That is because these are the only goddesses; all the rest are pure myth.

71

STREPSIADES: But by the Earth! is our father, Zeus, the Olympian, not a god?

SOCRATES: Zeus! what Zeus! Are you mad? There is no Zeus.

STREPSIADES: What are you saying now? Who causes the rain to fall? Answer me that!

SOCRATES: Why, these, and I will prove it. Have you ever seen it raining without clouds? Let Zeus then cause rain with a clear sky and without their presence!

STREPSIADES: By Apollo! that is powerfully argued! For my own part, I always thought it was Zeus pissing into a sieve. But tell me, who is it makes the thunder, which I so much dread?

SOCRATES: These, when they roll one over the other.

STREPSIADES: But how can that be? you most daring among men!

SOCRATES: Being full of water, and forced to move along, they are of necessity precipitated in rain, being fully distended with moisture from the regions where they have been floating; hence they bump each other heavily and burst with great noise.

STREPSIADES: But is it not Zeus who forces them to move?

SOCRATES: Not at all; it's the aerial Whirlwind.

STREPSIADES: The Whirlwind! ah! I did not know that. So Zeus, it seems, has no existence, and its the Whirlwind that reigns in his stead? But you have not yet told me what makes the roll of the thunder?

SOCRATES: Have you not understood me then? I tell you, that the Clouds, when full of rain, bump against one another, and that, being inordinately swollen out, they burst with a great noise.

STREPSIADES: How can you make me credit that?

SOCRATES: Take yourself as an example. When you have heartily gorged on stew at the Panathenaea, you get throes of stomach-ache and then suddenly your belly resounds with prolonged rumbling.

STREPSIADES: Yes, yes, by Apollo I suffer, I get colic, then the stew sets to rumbling like thunder and finally bursts forth with a terrific noise. At first, it's but a little gurgling pappax, pappax! then it increases, papapappax! and when I take my crap, why, it's thunder indeed, papapappax! pappax!! papapappax!!! just like the clouds.

SOCRATES: Well then, reflect what a noise is produced by your belly, which is but small. Shall not the air, which is boundless, produce these mighty claps of thunder?

STREPSIADES: And this is why the names are so much alike: crap and clap. But tell me this. Whence comes the lightning, the dazzling flame, which at times consumes the man it strikes, at others hardly singes him. Is it not plain, that Zeus is hurling it at the perjurers?

SOCRATES: Out upon the fool! the driveller! he still savours of the golden age! If Zeus strikes at the perjurers, why has he not blasted Simon, Cleonymus and Theorus? Of a surety, greater perjurers cannot exist. No, he strikes his own temple, and Sunium, the promontory of Athens, and the towering oaks. Now, why should he do that? An oak is no perjurer.

STREPSIADES: I cannot tell, but it seems to me well argued. What is the lightning then?

SOCRATES: When a dry wind ascends to the Clouds and gets shut into them, it blows them out like a bladder; finally, being too confined, it bursts them, escapes with fierce violence and a roar to flash into flame by reason of its own impetuosity.

STREPSIADES: Ah, that's just what happened to me one day. It was at the feast of Zeus! I was cooking a sow's belly for my family and I had forgotten to slit it open. It swelled out and, suddenly bursting, discharged itself right into my eyes and burnt my face.

LEADER OF THE CHORUS: Oh, mortal, you who desire to instruct yourself in our great wisdom, the Athenians, the Greeks will envy you your good fortune. Only you must have the memory and ardour for study, you must know how to stand the tests, hold your own, go forward without feeling fatigue, caring but little for food, abstaining from wine, gymnastic exercises and other similar follies, in fact, you must believe as every man of intellect should, that the greatest of all blessings is to live and think more clearly than the vulgar herd, to shine in the contests of words.

STREPSIADES: If it be a question of hardiness for labour, of spending whole nights at work, of living sparingly, of fighting my stomach and only eating chickpease, rest assured, I am as hard as an anvil.

SOCRATES: Henceforward, following our example, you will recognize no other gods but Chaos, the Clouds and the Tongue, these three alone.

STREPSIADES: I would not speak to the others, even if I met them in the street; not a single sacrifice, not a libation, not a grain of incense for them!

LEADER OF THE CHORUS: Tell us boldly then what you want of us; you cannot fail to succeed. If you honour and revere us and if you are resolved to become a clever man.

TRESPSIADES: Oh, sovereign goddesses, it is only a very small favour that I ask of you; grant that I may outdistance all the Greeks by a hundred stadia in the art of speaking.

LEADER OF THE CHORUS: We grant you this, and henceforward no eloquence shall more often succeed with the people than your own.

STREPSIADES: May the gods shield me from possessing great eloquence! That's not what I want. I want to be able to turn bad law-suits to my own advantage and to slip through the fingers of my creditors.

LEADER OF THE CHORUS: It shall be as you wish, for your ambitions are modest. Commit yourself fearlessly to our ministers, the sophists.

STREPSIADES: This I will do, for I trust in you. Moreover there is no drawing back, what with these cursed horses and this marriage, which has eaten up my vitals. (More and more volubly from here to the end of speeck) So let them do with me as they will; I yield my body to them. Come blows, come hunger, thirst, heat or cold, little matters it to me; they may flay me, if I only escape my debts, if only I win the reputation of being a bold rascal, a fine speaker, impudent, shameless, a braggart, and adept at stringing lies, an old stager at quibbles, a complete table of laws, a thorough rattle, a fox to slip through any hole; supple as a leathern strap, slippery as an eel, an artful fellow, a blusterer, a villain; a knave with a hundred faces, cunning, intolerable, a gluttonous dog. With such epithets do I seek to be greeted; on these terms they can treat me as they choose, and, if they wish, by Demeter! they can turn me into sausages and serve me up to the philosophers.

CHORUS: (singing) Here have we a bold and well-disposed pupil indeed. When we have taught you, your glory among the mortals will reach even to the skies.

STREPSIADES: (singing) Wherein will that profit me?

CHORUS: (singing) You will pass your whole life among us and will be the most envied of men.

STREPSIADES: (singing) Shall I really ever see such happiness?

CHORUS: (singing)   Clients will be everlastingly besieging your door in crowds, burning to get at you, to explain their business to you and to consult you about their suits, which, in return for your ability, will bring you in great sums.

LEADER OF THE CHORUS: But, Socrates, begin the lessons you want to teach this old man; rouse his mind, try the strength of his intelligence.

SOCRATES: Come, tell me the kind of mind you have; it's important that I know this, that I may order my batteries against you in the right fashion.

STREPSIADES: Eh, what! in the name of the gods, are you purposing to assault me then?

SOCRATES: No. I only wish to ask you some questions. Have you any memory?

STREPSIADES: That depends: if anything is owed me, my memory is excellent, but if I owe, alas! I have none whatever.

SOCRATES: Have you a natural gift for speaking?

STREPSIADES: For speaking, no; for cheating, yes.

SOCRATES: How will you be able to learn then?

STREPSIADES: Very easily, have no fear.

SOCRATES: Thus, when I throw forth some philosophical thought anent things celestial., you will seize it in its very flight?

STREPSIADES: Then I am to snap up wisdom much as a dog snaps up a morsel?

SOCRATES: (aside) Oh! the ignoramus! the barbarian! (to Strepsiades) I greatly fear, old man, it will be necessary for me to have recourse to blows. Now, let me hear what you do when you are beaten.

STREPSIADES: I receive the blow, then wait a moment, take my witnesses and finally summon my assailant at law.

SOCRATES: Come, take off your cloak.
STREPSIADES: Have I robbed you of anything?

SOCRATES: No. but the usual thing is to enter the school without your cloak.

STREPSIADES: But I have not come here to look for stolen goods.

SOCRATES: Off with it, fool!

STREPSIADES: (He obeys.) Tell me, if I prove thoroughly attentive and learn with zeal, which O; your disciples shall I resemble, do you think?

SOCRATES: You will be the image of Chaerephon.

STREPSIADES: Ah! unhappy me! Shall I then be only half alive?

SOCRATES: A truce to this chatter! follow me and no more of it.

STREPSIADES: First give me a honey-cake, for to descend down there sets me all a-tremble; it looks like the cave of Trophonius.

SOCRATES: But get in with you! What reason have you for thus dallying at the door? (They go into the Thoughtery.)

LEADER OF THE CHORUS: Good luck! you have courage; may you succeed, you, who, though already so advanced in years, wish to instruct your mind with new studies and practise it in wisdom! (The CHORUS turns and faces the Audience.) Spectators! By Bacchus, whose servant I am, I will frankly tell

77

you the truth. May I secure both victory and renown as certainly as I hold you for adept critics and as I regard this comedy as my best. I wished to give you the first view of a work, which had cost me much trouble, but which I withdrew, unjustly beaten by unskilful rivals. It is you, oh, enlightened public, for whom I have prepared my piece, that I reproach with this. Nevertheless I shall never willingly cease to seek the approval of the discerning. I have not forgotten the day, when men, whom one is happy to have for an audience, received my Virtuous Young Man and my Paederast with so much favour in this very place. Then as yet virgin, my Muse had not attained the age for maternity; she had to expose her first-born for another to adopt, and it has since grown up under your generous patronage. Ever since you have as good as sworn me your faithful alliance. Thus, like the Electra of the poets, my comedy has come to seek you to-day, hoping again to encounter such enlightened spectators. As far away as she can discern her Orestes, she will be able to recognize him by his curly head. And note her modest demeanour! She has not sewn on a piece of hanging leather, thick and reddened at the end, to cause laughter among the children; she does not rail at the bald, neither does she dance the cordax; no old man is seen, who, while uttering his lines, batters his questioner with a stick to make his poor jests pass muster. She does not rush upon the scene carrying a torch and screaming, 'Iou! Iou!' No, she relies upon herself and her verses....My value is so well known, that I take no further pride in it. I do not seek to deceive you, by reproducing the same subjects two or three times; I always invent fresh themes to present before you, themes that have no relation to each other and that are all clever. I attacked Cleon to his face and when he was all-powerful; but he has fallen, and now I have no desire to kick him when he is down. My rivals, on the contrary, now that this wretched Hyperbolus has given them the cue, have never ceased setting upon both him and his mother. First Eupolis presented his 'Maricas'; this was simply my 'Knights,' whom this plagiarist had clumsily furbished up again by adding to the piece an old drunken woman, so that she might dance the cordax. It was an old idea, taken from Phrynichus, who caused his old hag to be devoured by a monster of the deep. Then Hermippus fell foul of Hyperbolus and now all the others fall upon him and repeat my comparison of the eels. May those who find amusement in their pieces not be pleased with mine, but as for you, who love and applaud my inventions, why, posterity will praise your good taste.

FIRST SEMI-CHORUS: (singing) Oh, ruler of Olympus, all-powerful king of the gods, great Zeus, it is thou whom I first invoke; protect this chorus; and thou too, Posidon, whose dread trident upheaves at the will of thy anger both the bowels of the earth and the salty waves of the ocean. I invoke my illustrious father, the divine Aether, the universal sustainer of life, and Phoebus, who, from the summit of his chariot, sets the world aflame with his dazzling rays, Phoebus, a mighty deity amongst the gods and adored amongst mortals.

LEADER OF FIRST SEMI-CHORUS: Most wise spectators, lend us all your attention. Give heed to our just reproaches. There exist no gods to whom this city owes more than it does to us, whom alone you forget. Not a sacrifice, not a libation is there for those who protect you! Have you decreed some mad expedition? Well! we thunder or we fall down in rain. When you chose that enemy of heaven, the Paphlagonian tanner, for a general, we knitted our brow, we caused our wrath to break out; the lightning shot forth, the thunder pealed, the moon deserted her course and the sun at once veiled his beam threatening, no longer to give you light, if Cleon became general. Nevertheless you elected him; it is said, Athens never resolves upon some fatal step but the gods turn these errors into her greatest gain. Do you wish that his election should even now be a success for you? It is a very simple thing to do; condemn this rapacious gull named Cleon for bribery and extortion, fit a wooden collar tight round his neck, and your error will be rectified and the commonweal will at once regain its old prosperity.

SECOND SEMI-CHORUS: (singing) Aid me also, Phoebus, god of Delos, who reignest on the cragged peaks of Cynthia; and thou, happy virgin, to whom the Lydian damsels offer pompous sacrifice in a temple; of gold; and thou, goddess of our country, Athene, armed with the aegis, the protectress of Athens; and thou, who, surrounded by the bacchants of Delphi; roamest over the rocks of Parnassus shaking the flame of thy resinous torch, thou, Bacchus, the god of revel and joy.

LEADER OF SECOND SEMI-CHORUS: As we were preparing to come here, we were hailed by the Moon and were charged to wish joy and happiness both to the Athenians and to their allies; further, she said that she was enraged and that you treated her very shamefully, her, who does not pay you in words alone, but who renders you all real benefits. Firstly, thanks to her, you save at least a drachma each month for lights, for each, as he is leaving home at night, says, "Slave, buy no torches, for the moonlight is beautiful,"-not to name a thousand other benefits. Nevertheless you do not reckon the days correctly and your calendar is naught but confusion. Consequently the gods load her with threats each time they get home and are disappointed of their meal, because the festival has not been kept in the regular order of time. When you should be sacrificing, you are putting to the torture or administering justice. And often, we others, the gods, are fasting in token of mourning for the death of Memnon or Sarpedon, while you are devoting yourselves to joyous libations. It is for this, that last year, when the lot would have invested Hyperbolus with the duty of Amphictyon, we took his crown from him, to teach him that time must be divided according to the phases of the moon.

SOCRATES: (coming out) By Respiration, the Breath of Life! By Chaos! By the Air! I have never seen a man so gross, so inept, so stupid, so forgetful. All the little quibbles, which I teach him, he forgets even before he has learnt them. Yet I will not give it up, I will make him come out here into the open air. Where are you, Strepsiades? Come, bring your couch out here.

STREPSIADES: (from within) But the bugs will not allow me to bring it.

SOCRATES: Have done with such nonsense! place it there and pay attention.

STREPSIADES: (coming out, with the bed) Well, here I am.

SOCRATES: Good! Which science of all those you have never been taught, do you wish to learn first? The measures, the rhythms or the verses?

STREPSIADES: Why, the measures; the flour dealer cheated me out of two choenixes the other day.

SOCRATES: It's not about that I ask you, but which, according to you, is the best measure, the trimeter or the tetrameter?

STREPSIADES: The one I prefer is the semisextarius.

SOCRATES: You talk nonsense, my good fellow.

STREPSIADES: I will wager your tetrameter is the semisextarius.

SOCRATES: Plague seize the dunce and the fool! Come, perchance you will learn the rhythms quicker.

STREPSIADES: Will the rhythms supply me with food?

SOCRATES: First they will help you to be pleasant in company, then to know what is meant by enhoplian rhythm and what by the dactylic.

STREPSIADES: Of the dactyl? I know that quite well.

SOCRATES: What is it then, other than this finger here?

STREPSIADES: Formerly, when a child, I used this one.

SOCRATES: You are as low-minded as you are stupid.

STREPSIADES: But, wretched man, I do not want to learn all this.

SOCRATES: Then what do you want to know?

STREPSIADES: Not that, not that, but the art of false reasoning.

SOCRATES: But you must first learn other things. Come, what are the male quadrupeds?

STREPSIADES: Oh! I know the males thoroughly. Do you take me for a fool then? The ram, the buck, the bull, the dog, the pigeon.

SOCRATES: Do you see what you are doing; is not the female pigeon called the same as the male?

STREPSIADES: How else? Come now!

SOCRATES: How else? With you then it's pigeon and pigeon!

STREPSIADES: That's right, by Posidon! but what names do you want me to give them?

SOCRATES: Term the female pigeonnette and the male pigeon.

STREPSIADES: Pigeonnette! hah! by the Air! That's splendid! for that lesson bring out your kneading-trough and I will fill him with flour to the brim.

SOCRATES: There you are wrong again; you make trough masculine and it should be feminine.

STREPSIADES: What? if I say, him, do I make the trough masculine?
SOCRATES: Assuredly! would you not say him for Cleonymus?

STREPSIADES: Well?

SOCRATES: Then trough is of the same gender as Cleonymus?

STREPSIADES: My good man! Cleonymus never had a kneading-trough; he used a round mortar for the purpose. But come, tell me what I should say!

SOCRATES: For trough you should say her as you would for Soctrate.

STREPSIADES: Her?

SOCRATES: In this manner you make it truly female.

STREPSIADES: That's it! Her for trough and her for Cleonymus.

SOCRATES," Now I must teach you to distinguish the masculine proper names from those that are feminine.

STREPSIADES: Ah! I know the female names well.

SOCRATES: Name some then.

STREPSIADES: Lysilla, Philinna, Clitagora, Demetria.

SOCRATES: And what are masculine names?

STREPSIADES: They are are countless-Philoxenus, Melesias, Amynias.

SOCRATES: But, wretched man, the last two are not masculine.

STREPSIADES: You do not count them as masculine?

SOCRATES: Not at all. If you met Amynias, how would you hail him?

STREPSIADES: How? Why, I should shout, "Hi, there, Amynia!

SOCRATES: Do you see? it's a female name that you give him.

STREPSIADES: And is it not rightly done, since he refuses military service? But what use is there in learning what we all know?

SOCRATES: You know nothing about it. Come, lie down there.

STREPSIADES: What for?

SOCRATES: Ponder awhile over matters that interest you.

STREPSIADES: Oh! I pray you, not there but, if I must lie down and ponder, let me lie on the ground.

SOCRATES: That's out of the question. Come! on the couch!

STREPSIADES: (as he lies down) What cruel fate! What a torture the bugs will this day put me to! (SOCRATES: turns aside.)

CHORUS: (singing) Ponder and examine closely, gather your thoughts together, let your mind turn to every side of things; if you meet with a difficulty, spring quickly to some other idea; above all, keep your eyes away from all gentle sleep.

STREPSIADES: (singing) Ow, Wow, Wow, Wow is me!

CHORUS: (singing) What ails you? why do you cry so?

STREPSIADES: Oh! I am a dead man! Here are these cursed Corinthians advancing upon me from all corners of the couch; they are biting me, they are gnawing at my sides, they are drinking all my blood, they are yanking of my balls, they are digging into my arse, they are killing me!

LEADER OF THE CHORUS: Not so much wailing and clamour, if you please.

STREPSIADES: How can I obey? I have lost my money and my complexion, my blood and my slippers, and to cap my misery, I must keep awake on this couch, when scarce a breath of life is left in me. (A brief interval of silence ensues.)

SOCRATES: Well now! what are you doing? are you reflecting?

STREPSIADES: Yes, by Posidon!

SOCRATES: What about?

STREPSIADES: Whether the bugs will entirely devour me.

SOCRATES: May death seize you, accursed man! (He turns aside again.)

STREPSIADES: Ah it has already.

SOCRATES: Come, no giving way! Cover up your head; the thing to do is to find an ingenious alternative.

STREPSIADES: An alternative! ah! I only wish one would come to me from within these coverlets! (Another interval of silence ensues.)

SOCRATES: Wait! let us see what our fellow is doing! Ho! are you asleep?

STREPSIADES: No, by Apollo!

SOCRATES: Have you got hold of anything?

STREPSIADES: No, nothing whatever.

SOCRATES: Nothing at all?

STREPSIADES: No, nothing except my tool, which I've got in my hand.

SOCRATES: Aren't you going to cover your head immediately and ponder?

STREPSIADES: On what? Come, Socrates, tell me.

SOCRATES: Think first what you want, and then tell me.

STREPSIADES: But I have told you a thousand times what I want. Not to pay any of my creditors.

SOCRATES: Come, wrap yourself up; concentrate your mind, which wanders to lightly; study every detail, scheme and examine thoroughly.

STREPSIADES: Alas! Alas!

SOCRATES: Keep still, and if any notion troubles you, put it quickly aside, then resume it and think over it again.

STREPSIADES: My dear little Socrates!

SOCRATES: What is it, old greybeard?

STREPSIADES: I have a scheme for not paying my debts.

SOCRATES: Let us hear it.

STREPSIADES: Tell me, if I purchased a Thessalian witch, I could make the moon descend during the night and shut it, like a mirror, into a round box and there keep it carefully....

SOCRATES: How would you gain by that?

STREPSIADES: How? why, if the moon did not rise, I would have no interest to pay.

SOCRATES: Why so?

STREPSIADES: Because money is lent by the month.

SOCRATES: Good! but I am going to propose another trick to you. If you were condemned to pay five talents, how would you manage to quash that verdict? Tell me.

STREPSIADES: How? how? I don't know, I must think.

SOCRATES: Do you always shut your thoughts within yourself? Let your ideas fly in the air, like a may-bug, tied by the foot with a thread.

STREPSIADES: I have found a very clever way to annul that conviction; you will admit that much yourself.

SOCRATES: What is it?

STREPSIADES: Have you ever seen a beautiful, transparent stone at the druggists', with which you may kindle fire?

SOCRATES: You mean a crystal lens.

STREPSIADES: That's right. Well, now if I placed myself with this stone in the sun and a long way off from the clerk, while he was writing out the conviction, I could make all the wax, upon which the words were written, melt.

SOCRATES: Well thought out, by the Graces!

STREPSIADES: Ah! I am delighted to have annulled the decree that was to cost me five talents.

SOCRATES: Come, take up this next question quickly.

STREPSIADES: Which?

SOCRATES: If, when summoned to court, you were in danger of losing your case for want of witnesses, how would you make the conviction fall upon your opponent?

STREPSIADES: That's very simple and easy.

SOCRATES: Let me hear.

STREPSIADES: This way. If another case had to be pleaded before mine was called, I should run and hang myself.

SOCRATES: You talk rubbish!

STREPSIADES: Not so, by the gods! if I were dead, no action could lie against me.

SOCRATES: You are merely beating the air. Get out! I will give you no more lessons.

STREPSIADES: (imploringly) Why not? Oh! Socrates! in the name of the gods!

SOCRATES: But you forget as fast as you learn. Come, what was the thing I taught you first? Tell me.

STREPSIADES: Ah let me see. What was the first thing? What was it then? Ah! that thing in which we knead the bread, oh! my god! what do you call it?

SOCRATES: Plague take the most forgetful and silliest of old addlepates!

STREPSIADES: Alas! what a calamity! what will become of me? I am undone if I do not learn how to ply my tongue. Oh! Clouds! give me good advice.

CHORUS-LEADER: Old man, we counsel you, if you have brought up a son, to send him to learn in your stead.

STREPSIADES: Undoubtedly I have a son, as well endowed as the best, but he is unwilling to learn. What will become of me?

CHORUS-LEADER: And you don't make him obey you?

STREPSIADES: You see, he is big and strong; moreover, through his mother he is a descendant of those fine birds, the race of Coesyra. Nevertheless, I will go and find him, and if he refuses, I will turn him out of the house. Go in, Socrates, and wait for me awhile. (Socrates goes into the Thoughtery, Strepsiades into his own house.)

CHORUS: (singing) Do you understand, Socrates, that thanks to us you will be loaded with benefits? Here is a man, ready to obey you in all things. You see how he is carried away with admiration and enthusiasm. Profit by it to clip him as short as possible; fine chances are all too quickly gone.

STREPSIADES: (coming out of his house and pushing his son in front of him) No, by the Clouds! you stay here no longer; go and devour the ruins of your uncle Megacles' fortune.

PHIDIPPIDES: Oh! my poor father! what has happened to you? By the Olympian Zeus! You are no longer in your senses!

STREPSIADES: Look! "the Olympian Zeus." Oh! you fool! to believe in Zeus at your age!

PHIDIPPIDES: What is there in that to make you laugh?

STREPSIADES: You are then a tiny little child, if you credit such antiquated rubbish! But come here, that I may teach you; I will tell you something very necessary to know to be a man; but do not repeat it to anybody.

PHIDIPPIDES: Tell me, what is it?

STREPSIADES: Just now you swore by Zeus.

PHIDIPPIDES: Sure I did.

STREPSIADES: Do you see how good it is to learn? Phidippides, there is no Zeus.

PHIDIPPIDES: What is there then?

STREPSIADES: The Whirlwind has driven out Zeus and is King now.

PHIDIPPIDES: What drivel!

STREPSIADES: You must realize that it is true.

PHIDIPPIDES: And who says so?

STREPSIADES: Socrates, the Melian, and Chaerephon, who knows how to measure the jump of a flea.

PHIDIPPIDES: Have you reached such a pitch of madness that you believe those bilious fellows?

STREPSIADES: Use better language, and do not insult men who are clever and full of wisdom, who, to economize, never shave, shun the gymnasia and never go to the baths, while you, you only await my death to eat up my wealth. But come, come as quickly as you can to learn in my stead.

PHIDIPPIDES: And what good can be learnt of them?

STREPSIADES: What good indeed? Why, all human knowledge. Firstly, you will know yourself grossly ignorant. But await me here awhile. (He goes back into his house.)

PHIDIPPIDES: Alas! what is to be done? Father has lost his wits. Must I have him certificated for lunacy, or must I order his coffin?

STREPSIADES: (returning with a bird in each hand) Come! what kind of bird is this? Tell me.

PHIDIPPIDES: A pigeon.

STREPSIADES: Good! And this female?

PHIDIPPIDES: A pigeon.

STREPSIADES: The same for both? You make me laugh! In the future you must call this one a pigeonnette and the other a pigeon.

PHIDIPPIDES: A pigeonnette! These then are the fine things you have just learnt at the school of these sons of Earth!

STREPSIADES: And many others; but what I learnt I forgot at once, because I am to old.

PHIDIPPIDES: So this is why you have lost your cloak?

STREPSIADES: I have not lost it, I have consecrated it to Philosophy.

PHIDIPPIDES: And what have you done with your sandals, you poor fool?

STREPSIADES: If I have lost them, it is for what was necessary, just as Pericles did. But come, move yourself, let us go in; if necessary, do wrong to obey your father. When you were six years old and still lisped, I was the one who obeyed you. I remember at the feasts of Zeus you had a consuming wish for a little chariot and I bought it for you with the first obolus which I received as a juryman in the courts.

PHIDIPPIDES: You will soon repent of what you ask me to do.

STREPSIADES: Oh! now I am happy! He obeys. (loudly) Come, Socrates, come! Come out quick! Here I am bringing you my son; he refused, but I have persuaded him.

SOCRATES: Why, he is but a child yet. He is not used to these baskets, in which we suspend our minds.

PHIDIPPIDES: To make you better used to them, I would you were hung.

STREPSIADES: A curse upon you! you insult your master!

SOCRATES: "I would you were hung!" What a stupid speech! and so emphatically spoken! How can one ever get out of an accusation with such a tone, summon witnesses or touch or convince? And yet when we think, Hyperbolus learnt all this for one talent!

STREPSIADES: Rest undisturbed and teach him. He has a most intelligent nature. Even when quite little he amused himself at home with making houses, carving boats, constructing little chariots of leather, and understood wonderfully how to make frogs out of pomegranate rinds. Teach him both methods of reasoning, the strong and also the weak, which by false arguments triumphs over the strong; if not the two, at least the false, and that in every possible way.

SOCRATES: The Just and Unjust Discourse : themselves shall instruct him. I shall leave you.

STREPSIADES: But forget it not, he must always, always be able to confound the true. (Socrates enters the Thoughtery; a moment later the Just and the Unjust Discourse come out; they are quarrelling violently.)

JUST DISCOURSE: Come here! Shameless as you may be, will you dare to show your face to the spectators?

UNJUST DISCOURSE: Take me where you will. I seek a throng, so that I may the better annihilate you.

JUST DISCOURSE: Annihilate me! Do you forget who you are?

UNJUST DISCOURSE: I am Reasoning.

JUST DISCOURSE: Yes, the weaker Reasoning."

UNJUST DISCOURSE: But I triumph over you, who claim to be the stronger.

JUST DISCOURSE: By what cunning shifts, pray?

UNJUST DISCOURSE: By the invention of new maxims.

JUST DISCOURSE: .... which are received with favour by these fools. (He points to the audience.)

UNJUST DISCOURSE: Say rather, by these wise men.

JUST DISCOURSE: I am going to destroy you mercilessly.

UNJUST DISCOURSE: How pray? Let us see you do it.

JUST DISCOURSE: By saying what is true.

UNJUST DISCOURSE: I shall retort and shall very soon have the better of you. First, maintain that justice has no existence.

JUST DISCOURSE: Has no existence?

UNJUST DISCOURSE: No existence! Why, where is it?

JUST DISCOURSE: With the gods.

UNJUST DISCOURSE: How then, if justice exists, was Zeus not put to death for having put his father in chains?

JUST DISCOURSE: Bah! this is enough to turn my stomach! A basin, quick!

UNJUST DISCOURSE: You are an old driveller and stupid withal.

JUST DISCOURSE: And you a degenerate and shameless fellow.

UNJUST DISCOURSE: Hah! What sweet expressions!

JUST DISCOURSE: An impious buffoon.

UNJUST DISCOURSE: You crown me with roses and with lilies.

JUST DISCOURSE: A Parricide.

UNJUST DISCOURSE: Why, you shower gold upon me.

JUST DISCOURSE: Formerly it was a hailstorm of blows.

UNJUST DISCOURSE: I deck myself with your abuse.

JUST DISCOURSE: What impudence!

UNJUST DISCOURSE: What tomfoolery!

JUST DISCOURSE: It is because of you that the youth no longer attends the schools. The Athenians will soon recognize what lessons you teach those who are fools enough to believe you.

UNJUST DISCOURSE: You are overwhelmed with wretchedness.

JUST DISCOURSE: And you, you prosper. Yet you were poor when you said, "I am the Mysian Telephus," and used to stuff your wallet with maxims of Pandeletus to nibble at.

UNJUST DISCOURSE: Oh! the beautiful wisdom, of which you are now boasting!

JUST DISCOURSE: Madman! But yet madder the city that keeps you, you, the corrupter of its youth!

UNJUST DISCOURSE: It is not you who will teach this young man; you are as old and out of date at Cronus.

JUST DISCOURSE: Nay, it will certainly be I, if he does not wish to be lost and to practise verbosity only.

UNJUST DISCOURSE: (to PHIDIPPIDES) Come here and leave him to beat the air.

JUST DISCOURSE: You'll regret it, if you touch him.

CHORUS-LEADER: (stepping between them as they are about to come to blows) A truce to your quarrellings and abuse! But you expound what you taught us formerly, and you, your new doctrine. Thus, after hearing each of you argue, he will be able to choose betwixt the two schools.

JUST DISCOURSE: I am quite agreeable.

UNJUST DISCOURSE: And I too.

LEADER OF THE CHORUS: Who is to speak first?

UNJUST DISCOURSE: Let it be my opponent, he has my full consent; then I shall follow upon the very ground he shall have chosen and shall shatter him with a hail of new ideas and subtle fancies; if after that he dares to breathe another word, I shall sting him in the face and in the eyes with our maxims, which are as keen as the sting of a wasp, and he will die.

CHORUS: (singing) Here are two rivals confident in their powers of oratory and in the thoughts over which they have pondered so long. Let us see which will come triumphant out of the contest. This wisdom, for which my friends maintain such a persistent fight, is in great danger.

LEADER OF THE CHORUS: Come then, you, who crowned men of other days with so many virtues, plead the cause dear to you, make yourself known to us.

JUST DISCOURSE: Very well, I will tell you what was the old education, when I used to teach justice with so much success and when modesty was held in veneration. Firstly, it was required of a child, that it should not utter a word. In the street, when they went to the music-school, all the youths of the same district marched lightly clad and ranged in good order, even when the snow was falling in great flakes. At the   master's house they had to stand with their legs apart and they were taught to sing either, "Pallas, the Terrible, who overturneth cities," or "A noise resounded from afar" in the solemn tones of the ancient harmony. If anyone indulged in buffoonery or lent his voice any of the soft inflexions, like those which to-day the disciples of Phrynis take so much pains to form, he was treated as an enemy of the Muses and belaboured with blows. In the wrestling school they would sit with outstretched legs and without display of any indecency to the curious. When they rose, they would smooth over the sand, so as to leave no trace to excite obscene thoughts. Never was a child rubbed with oil below the belt; the rest of their bodies thus retained its fresh bloom and down, like a velvety peach. They were not to be seen approaching a lover and themselves rousing his passion by soft modulation of the voice and lustful gaze. At table, they would not have dared, before those older than themselves, to have

95

taken a radish, an aniseed or a leaf of parsley, and much less eat fish or thrushes or cross their legs.

UNJUST DISCOURSE: What antiquated rubbish! Have we got back to the days of the festivals of Zeus Polieus, to the Buphonia, to the time of the poet Cecides and the golden cicadas?

JUST DISCOURSE: Nevertheless by suchlike teaching I built up the men of Marathon-But you, you teach the children of to-day to bundle themselves quickly into their clothes, and I am enraged when I see them at the Panathenaea forgetting Athene while they dance, and covering their tools with their bucklers. Hence, young man, dare to range yourself beside me, who follow justice and truth; you will then be able to shun the public place, to refrain from the baths, to blush at all that is shameful, to fire up if your virtue is mocked at, to give place to your elders, to honour your parents, in short, to avoid all that is evil. Be modesty itself, and do not run to applaud the dancing girls; if you delight in such scenes, some courtesan will cast you her apple and your reputation will be done for. Do not bandy words with your father, nor treat him as a dotard, nor reproach the old man, who has cherished you, with his age.

UNJUST DISCOURSE: If you listen to him, by Bacchus! you will be the image of the sons of Hippocrates and will be called mother's big ninny.

JUST DISCOURSE: No, but you will pass your days at the gymnasia, glowing with   strength and health; you will not go to the public place to cackle and wrangle as is done nowadays; you will not live in fear that you may be dragged before the courts for some trifle exaggerated by quibbling. But you will go down to the Academy to run beneath the sacred olives with some virtuous friend of your own age, your head encircled with the white reed, enjoying your ease and breathing the perfume of the yew and of the fresh sprouts of the poplar, rejoicing in the return of springtide and gladly listening to the gentle rustle of the plane tree and the elm.

(With greater warmth from here on)

96

If you devote yourself to practising my precepts, your chest will be stout, your colour glowing, your shoulders broad, your tongue short, your hips muscular, but your tool small. But if you follow the fashions of the day, you will be pallid in hue, have narrow shoulders, a narrow chest, a long tongue, small hips and a big thing; you will know how to spin forth long-winded arguments on law. You will be persuaded also to regard as splendid everything that is shameful and as shameful everything that is honourable; in a word, you will wallow in degeneracy like Antimachus.

CHORUS: (singing) How beautiful, high-souled, brilliant is this wisdom that you practise! What a sweet odour of honesty is emitted by your discourse! Happy were those men of other days who lived when you were honoured! And you, seductive talker, come, find some fresh arguments, for your rival has done wonders.

LEADER OF THE CHORUS: You will have to bring out against him all the battery of your wit, it you desire to beat him and not to be laughed out of court.

UNJUST DISCOURSE: At last! I was choking with impatience, I was burning to upset his arguments! If I am called the Weaker Reasoning in the schools, it is just because I was the first to discover the means to confute the laws and the decrees of justice. To invoke solely the weaker arguments and yet triumph is an art worth more than a hundred thousand drachmae. But see how I shall batter down the sort of education of which he is so proud. Firstly, he forbids you to bathe in hot water. What grounds have you for condemning hot baths?

JUST DISCOURSE: Because they are baneful and enervate men.

UNJUST DISCOURSE: Enough said! Oh! you poor wrestler! From the very outset I have seized you and hold you round the middle; you cannot escape me. Tell me, of all the sons of Zeus, who had the stoutest heart, who performed the most doughty deeds?

JUST DISCOURSE: None, in my opinion, surpassed Heracles.

UNJUST DISCOURSE: Where have you ever seen cold baths called 'Bath of Heracles'? And yet who was braver than he?

JUST DISCOURSE: It is because of such quibbles, that the baths are seen crowded with young folk, who chatter there the livelong day while the gymnasia remain empty.

UNJUST DISCOURSE: Next you condemn the habit of frequenting the market-place, while I approve this. If it were wrong Homer would never have made Nestor speak in public as well as all his wise heroes. As for the art of speaking, he tells you, young men should not practise it; I hold the contrary. Furthermore he preaches chastity to them. Both precepts are equally harmful. Have you ever seen chastity of any use to anyone? Answer and try to confute me.

JUST DISCOURSE: To many; for instance, Peleus won a sword thereby.

UNJUST DISCOURSE: A sword! Ah! what a fine present to make him! Poor wretch! Hyperbolus, the lamp-seller, thanks to his villainy, has gained more than....do not know how many talents, but certainly no sword.

JUST DISCOURSE: Peleus owed it to his chastity that he became the husband of Thetis.

UNJUST DISCOURSE: .... who left him in the lurch, for he was not the most ardent; in those nocturnal sports between the sheets, which so please women, he possessed but little merit. Get you gone, you are but an old fool. But you, young man, just consider a little what this temperance means and the delights of which it deprives you-young fellows, women, play, dainty dishes, wine, boisterous laughter. And what is life worth without these? Then, if you happen to commit one of these faults inherent in human weakness, some seduction or adultery, and you are caught in the act, you are lost, if you cannot speak. But follow my teaching and you will be able to satisfy your passions, to dance, to laugh, to blush at nothing. Suppose you are caught in the act of adultery. Then up and tell the husband you are not guilty, and recall to him the example of Zeus, who

98

allowed himself to be conquered by love and by women. Being but a mortal, can you be stronger than a god?

JUST DISCOURSE: Suppose your pupil, following your advice, gets the radish rammed up his arse and then is depilated with a hot coal; how are you going to prove to him that he is not a broad-arse?

UNJUST DISCOURSE: What's the matter with being a broad-arse?

JUST DISCOURSE: Is there anything worse than that?

UNJUST DISCOURSE: Now what will you say, if I beat you even on this point?

JUST DISCOURSE: I should certainly have to be silent then.

UNJUST DISCOURSE: : Well then, reply! Our advocates, what are they?

JUST DISCOURSE: Sons of broad-arses.

UNJUST DISCOURSE: : Nothing is more true. And our tragic poets?

JUST DISCOURSE: Sons of broad-arses.

UNJUST DISCOURSE: : Well said again. And our demagogues?

JUST DISCOURSE: Sons of broad-arses.

UNJUST DISCOURSE: : You admit that you have spoken nonsense. And the spectators, what are they for the most part? Look at them.

JUST DISCOURSE: I am looking at them.

UNJUST DISCOURSE: : Well! What do you see?

JUST DISCOURSE: By the gods, they are nearly all broad-arses. (pointing) See, this one I know to be such and that one and that other with the long hair.

UNJUST DISCOURSE: :   What have you to say, then?

JUST DISCOURSE: I am beaten. Debauchees! in the name of the gods, receive my cloak; I pass over to your ranks. (He goes back into the Thoughtery.)

UNJUST DISCOURSE: :   Well then! Are you going to take away your son or do you wish me to teach him how to speak?

STREPSIADES: Teach him, chastise him and do not fail to sharpen his tongue well, on one side for petty law-suits and on the other for important cases.

UNJUST DISCOURSE: :   Don't worry, I shall return him to you an accomplished sophist.

PHIDIPPIDES: Very pale then and thoroughly hang-dog-looking.

LEADER OF THE CHORUS Take him with you. (The Unjust Discourse: and Phidippides go into the Thoughtery. To Strepsiades, who is just going into his own house.)   I think you will regret this. (The CHORUS turns and faces the audience.) judges, we are all about to tell you what you will gain by awarding us the crown as equity requires of you. In spring, when you wish to give your fields the first dressing, we will rain upon you first; the others shall wait. Then we will watch over your corn and over your vinestocks; they will have no excess to fear, neither of heat nor of wet. But if a mortal dares to insult the goddesses of the Clouds, let him think of the ills we shall pour upon him. For him neither wine nor any harvest at all! Our terrible slings will mow down his young olive plants and his vines. If he is making bricks, it will rain, and our round hailstones will break the tiles of his roof. If he himself marries or any of his relations or friends, we shall cause rain to fall the whole night long. Verily, he would prefer to live in Egypt than to have given this iniquitous verdict. **STREPSIADES**: (coming out again) Another four, three, two days, then the eve, then the day, the fatal day of payment! I tremble, I quake, I shudder, for it's the day of the old moon and the new. Then all my creditors take the oath, pay their deposits, I swear my downfall

100

and my ruin. As for me, I beseech them to be reasonable, to be just, "My friend, do not demand this sum, wait a little for this other and give me time for this third one." Then they will pretend that at this rate they will never be repaid, will accuse me of bad faith and will threaten me with the law. Well then, let them sue me! I care nothing for that, if only Phidippides has learnt to speak fluently. I am going to find out; I'll knock at the door of the school. (He knocks.).... Ho! slave, slave!

SOCRATES: (coming out) Welcome! Strepsiades!

STREPSIADES: Welcome! Socrates! But first take this sack (offers him a sack of flour); it is right to reward the master with some present. And my son, whom you took off lately, has he learnt this famous reasoning? Tell me.

SOCRATES: He has learnt it.

STREPSIADES: Wonderful! Oh! divine Knavery!

SOCRATES: You will win just as many causes as you choose.

STREPSIADES: Even if I have borrowed before witnesses?

SOCRATES: So much the better, even if there are a thousand of them!

STREPSIADES: (bursting into song) Then I am going to shout with all my might. "Woe to the usurers, woe to their capital and their interest and their compound interest! You shall play me no more bad turns. My son is being taught there, his tongue is being sharpened into a double-edged weapon; he is my defender, the saviour of my house, the ruin of my foes! His poor father was crushed down with misfortune and he delivers him." Go and call him to me quickly. Oh! my child! my dear little one! run forward to your father's voice!

SOCRATES: (singing) Lo, the man himself!

STREPSIADES: (singing) Oh, my friend, my dearest friend!

101

SOCRATES: (singing) Take your son, and get you gone.

STREPSIADES: (as Phidippides appears) Oh, my son! oh! oh! what a pleasure to see your pallor! You are ready first to deny and then to contradict; it's as clear as noon. What a child of your country you are! How your lips quiver with the famous, "What have you to say now?" How well you know, I am certain, to put on the look of a victim, when it is you who are making both victims and dupes! And what a truly Attic glance! Come, it's for you to save me, seeing it is you who have ruined me.

PHIDIPPIDES: What is it you fear then?

STREPSIADES: The day of the old and the new.

PHIDIPPIDES: Is there then a day of the old and the new?

STREPSIADES: The day on which they threaten to pay deposit against me.

PHIDIPPIDES: Then so much the worse for those who have deposited! for it's not possible for one day to be two.

STREPSIADES: What?

PHIDIPPIDES: Why, undoubtedly, unless a woman can be both old and young at the same time.

STREPSIADES: But so runs the law.

PHIDIPPIDES: I think the meaning of the law is quite misunderstood.

STREPSIADES: What does it mean?

PHIDIPPIDES: Old Solon loved the people.

STREPSIADES: What has that to do with the old day and the new?

PHIDIPPIDES: He has fixed two days for the summons, the last day of the old moon and the first day of the new; but the deposits must only be paid on the first day of the new moon.

STREPSIADES: And why did he also name the last day of the old?

PHIDIPPIDES: So, my dear sir, that the debtors, being there the day before, might free themselves by mutual agreement, or that else, if not, the creditor might begin his action on the morning of the new moon.

STREPSIADES: Why then do the magistrates have the deposits paid on the last of the month and not the next day?

PHIDIPPIDES: I think they do as the gluttons do, who are the first to pounce upon the dishes. Being eager to carry off these deposits, they have them paid in a day too soon.

STREPSIADES: Splendid! (to the audience) Ah! you poor brutes, who serve for food to us clever folk! You are only down here to swell the number, true blockheads, sheep for shearing, heap of empty pots! Hence I will sing a song of victory for my son and myself. "Oh! happy,

STREPSIADES: ! what cleverness is thine! and what a son thou hast here!" Thus my friends and my neighbours will say, jealous at seeing me gain all my suits. But come in, I wish to regale you first. (They both go in. A moment later a creditor arrives, with his witness.)

PASIAS: (to the Witness) A man should never lend a single obolus. It would be better to put on a brazen face at the outset than to get entangled in such matters. I want to see my money again and I bring you here to-day to attest the loan. I am going to make a foe of a neighbour; but, as long as I live, I do not wish my country to have to blush for me. Come, I am going to summon Strepsiades....

STREPSIADES: (coming out of his house) Who is this?

PASIAS: ....for the old day and the new.

STREPSIADES: (to the Witness) I call you to witness, that he has named two days. What do you want of me?

PASIAS: I claim of you the twelve minae, which you borrowed from me to buy the dapple-grey horse.

STREPSIADES: A horse! do you hear him? I, who detest horses, as is well known.

PASIAS: I call Zeus to witness, that you swore by the gods to return them to me.

STREPSIADES: Because at that time, by Zeus! Phidippides did not yet know the irrefutable argument.

PASIAS: Would you deny the debt on that account?

STREPSIADES: If not, what use is his science to me?

PASIAS: Will you dare to swear by the gods that you owe me nothing?

STREPSIADES: By which gods?

PASIAS: By Zeus, Hermes and Posidon!

STREPSIADES: Why, I would give three obols for the pleasure of swearing by them.

PASIAS: Woe upon you, impudent knave!

STREPSIADES: Oh! what a fine wine-skin you would make if flayed!

PASIAS: Heaven! he jeers at me!

STREPSIADES: It would hold six gallons easily.

PASIAS: By great Zeus! by all the gods! you shall not scoff at me with impunity,

STREPSIADES: Ah! how you amuse me with your gods! how ridiculous it seems to a sage to hear Zeus invoked.

PASIAS: Your blasphemies will one day meet their reward. But, come, will you repay me my money, yes or no? Answer me, that I may go.

STREPSIADES: Wait a moment, I am going to give you a distinct answer. (He goes indoors and returns immediately with a kneading-trough.)

PASIAS: (to the Witness) What do you think he will do? Do you think he will pay?

STREPSIADES: Where is the man who demands money? Tell me, what is this?

PASIAS: Him? Why, he is your kneading-trough. STREPSIADES: And you dare to demand money of me, when you are so ignorant? I will not return an obolus to anyone who says him instead of her for a kneading-trough.

PASIAS: You will not repay?

STREPSIADES: Not if I know it. Come, an end to this, pack off as quick as you can.

PASIAS: I go, but, may I die, if it be not to pay my deposit for a summons. (Exit)

STREPSIADES: Very well! It will be so much more loss to add to the twelve minae. But truly it makes me sad, for I do pity a poor simpleton who says him for a kneading-trough (Another creditor arrives.)

AMYNIAS: Woe! ah woe is me!

STREPSIADES: Wait! who is this whining fellow? Can it be one of the gods of Carcinus?

AMYNIAS: Do you want to know who I am? I am a man of misfortune!

STREPSIADES: Get on your way then.

AMYNIAS: (in tragic style)   Oh! cruel god! Oh Fate, who hast broken the wheels of my chariot! Oh, Pallas, thou hast undone me!

STREPSIADES: What ill has Tlepolemus done you?

AMYNIAS: Instead of jeering me, friend, make your son return me the money he has had of me; I am already unfortunate
enough.

STREPSIADES: What money?

AMYNIAS: The money he borrowed of me.

STREPSIADES: You have indeed had misfortune, it seems to me.

AMYNIAS: Yes, by the gods! I have been thrown from a chariot.

STREPSIADES: Why then drivel as if you had fallen off an ass?

AMYNIAS: Am I drivelling because I demand my money?

STREPSIADES: No, no, you cannot be in your right senses.

AMYNIAS: Why?

STREPSIADES: No doubt your poor wits have had a shake.

AMYNIAS: But by Hermes! I will sue you at law, if you do not pay me.

STREPSIADES: Just tell me; do you think it is always fresh water that Zeus lets fall every time it rains, or is ill always the same water that the sun pumps over the earth?

AMYNIAS: I neither know, nor care.

STREPSIADES: And actually you would claim the right to demand your money, when you know not an iota of these celestial phenomena?

AMYNIAS: If you are short, pay me the interest anyway.

STREPSIADES: What kind of animal is interest?

AMYNIAS: What? Does not the sum borrowed go on growing, growing every month, each day as the time slips by?

STREPSIADES: Well put. But do you believe there is more water in the sea now than there was formerly?

AMYNIAS: No, it's just the same quantity. It cannot increase. STREPSIADES: Thus, poor fool, the sea, that receives the rivers, never grows, and yet you would have your money grow? Get you gone, away with you, quick! Slave! bring me the ox-goad!

AMYNIAS: I have witnesses to this.

STREPSIADES: Come, what are you waiting for? Will you not budge, old nag!

AMYNIAS: What an insult!

STREPSIADES: Unless you start trotting, I shall catch you and stick this in your arse, you sorry packhorse! (AMYNIAS runs off.) Ah! you start, do you? I was about to drive you pretty fast, I tell you-you and your wheels and your chariot! (He enters his house.)

CHORUS: (singing) Whither does the passion of evil lead! here is a perverse old man, who wants to cheat his creditors; but some mishap, which will speedily punish this rogue for his shameful schemings, cannot fail to overtake him from to-day. For a long time he has been burning to have his son know how to fight against all justice and right and to gain even the most iniquitous causes against his adversaries every one. I think this wish is going to be fulfilled. But mayhap, mayhap, will he soon wish his son were dumb rather!

STREPSIADES: (rushing out With Phidippides after him) Oh! oh! Neighbours, kinsmen, fellow-citizens, help! help! to the rescue, I am being beaten! Oh! my head! oh! my jaw! Scoundrel! Do you beat your own father?

PHIDIPPIDES: (calmly) Yes, father, I do.

STREPSIADES: See! he admits he is beating me.

PHIDIPPIDES: Of course I do.

STREPSIADES: You villain, you PARRICIDE: , you gallows-bird!

PHIDIPPIDES: Go on, repeat your epithets, call me a thousand other names, if it please you. The more you curse, the greater my amusement!

STREPSIADES: Oh! you ditch-arsed cynic!

PHIDIPPIDES: How fragrant the perfume breathed forth in your words.

STREPSIADES: Do you beat your own father?

PHIDIPPIDES: Yes, by Zeus! and I am going to show you that I do right in beating you.

STREPSIADES: Oh, wretch! can it be right to beat a father?

PHIDIPPIDES: I will prove it to you, and you shall own yourself vanquished.

STREPSIADES: Own myself vanquished on a point like this?

PHIDIPPIDES: It's the easiest thing in the world. Choose whichever of the two reasonings you like.

STREPSIADES: Of which reasonings?

PHIDIPPIDES: The Stronger and the Weaker.

STREPSIADES: Miserable fellow! Why, I am the one who had you taught how to refute what is right. and now you would persuade me it is right a son should beat his father.

PHIDIPPIDES: I think I shall convince you so thoroughly that, when you have heard me, you will not have a word to say.

STREPSIADES: Well, I am curious to hear what you have to say.

CHORUS: (singing) Consider well, old man, how you can best
triumph over him. His brazenness shows me that he thinks himself sure of his case; he has some argument which gives him nerve. Note the confidence in his look!

LEADER OF THE CHORUS: But how did the fight begin? tell the Chorus; you cannot help doing that much.

STREPSIADES: I will tell you what was the start of the quarrel. At the end of the meal, as you know, I bade him take his lyre and sing me the air of Simonides, which tells of the fleece of the ram. He replied bluntly, that it was stupid, while drinking, to play the lyre and sing, like a woman when she is grinding barley.

PHIDIPPIDES: Why, by rights I ought to have beaten and kicked you the very moment you told me to sing I

STREPSIADES: That is just how he spoke to me in the house, furthermore he added, that Simonides was a detestable poet. However, I mastered myself and for a while said nothing. Then I said to him, 'At least, take a myrtle branch and recite a passage from Aeschylus to me.'-'For my own part,' he at once replied, 'I look upon Aeschylus as the first of poets, for his verses roll superbly; they're nothing but incoherence, bombast and turgidity.' Yet still I smothered my wrath and said, 'Then recite one of the famous pieces from the modern poets.' Then he commenced a piece in which Euripides shows, oh! horror! a brother, who violates his own uterine sister. Then I could not longer restrain myself, and attacked him with the most injurious abuse; naturally he retorted; hard words were hurled on both sides, and finally he sprang at me, broke my bones, bore me to
earth, strangled and started killing me!

PHIDIPPIDES: I was right. What! not praise Euripides, the greatest of our poets?

STREPSIADES: He the greatest of our poets? Ah! if I but dared to speak! but the blows would rain upon me harder than ever.

PHIDIPPIDES: Undoubtedly and rightly too.

STREPSIADES: Rightly! Oh! what impudence! to me, who brought you up! when you could hardly lisp, I guessed what you wanted. If you said broo, broo, well, I brought you your milk; if you asked for mam mam, I gave you bread; and you had no sooner said, caca, than I took you outside and held you out. And just now, when you were strangling me, I   shouted, I bellowed that I was about to crap; and you, you   scoundrel, had not the heart to take me outside, so that, though almost choking, I was compelled to do my crapping right there.

CHORUS: (singing) Young men, your hearts must be panting with impatience. What is

PHIDIPPIDES: going to say? If, after such conduct, he proves he has done well, I would not give an obolus for the hide of old men.

LEADER OF THE CHORUS: Come, you, who know how to brandish and hurl the keen shafts of the new science, find a way to convince us, give your language an appearance of truth.

PHIDIPPIDES: How pleasant it is to know these clever new inventions and to be able to defy the established laws! When I thought only about horses, I was not able to string three words together without a mistake, but now that the master has altered and improved me and that I live in this world of subtle thought, of reasoning and of meditation, I count on being able to prove satisfactorily that I have done well to thrash my father.

STREPSIADES: Mount your horse! By Zeus! I would rather defray the keep of a four-in-hand team than be battered with blows.

PHIDIPPIDES: I revert to what I was saying when you interrupted me. And first, answer me, did you beat me in my childhood?

STREPSIADES: Why, assuredly, for your good and in your own best interest.

PHIDIPPIDES: Tell me, is it not right, that in turn I should beat you for your good, since it is for a man's own best interest to be beaten? What! must your body be free of blows, and not mine? am I not free-born too? the children are to weep and the fathers go free? You will tell me, that according to the law, it is the lot of children to be beaten. But I reply that the old men are children twice over and that it is far more fitting to chastise them than the young, for there is less excuse for their faults.

STREPSIADES: But the law nowhere admits that fathers should be treated thus.

PHIDIPPIDES: Was not the legislator who carried this law a man like you and me? In those days be got men to believe him; then why should not I too have the right to establish for the future a new law, allowing children to beat their fathers in turn? We make you a present of all the blows which were received before his law, and admit that you thrashed us with impunity. But look how the

111

cocks and other animals fight with their fathers; and yet what difference is there betwixt them and ourselves, unless it be that they do not propose decrees?

STREPSIADES: But if you imitate the cocks in all things, why don't you scratch up the dunghill, why don't you sleep on a perch?

PHIDIPPIDES: That has no bearing on the case, good sir; Socrates would find no connection, I assure you.

STREPSIADES: Then do not beat at all, for otherwise you have only yourself to blame afterwards.

PHIDIPPIDES: What for?

STREPSIADES: I have the right to chastise you, and you to chastise your son, if you have one.

PHIDIPPIDES: And if I have not, I shall have cried in vain, and you will die laughing in my face.

STREPSIADES: What say you, all here present? It seems to me that he is right, and I am of opinion that they should be accorded their right. If we think wrongly, it is but just we should be beaten.

PHIDIPPIDES: Again, consider this other point.

STREPSIADES: It will be the death of me.

PHIDIPPIDES: But you will certainly feel no more anger because of the blows I have given you.

STREPSIADES: Come, show me what profit I shall gain from it.

PHIDIPPIDES: I shall beat my mother just as I have you.

STREPSIADES: What do you say? what's that you say? Hah! this is far worse still.

PHIDIPPIDES: And what if I prove to you by our school reasoning, that one ought to beat one's mother?

STREPSIADES: Ah! if you do that, then you will only have to throw yourself, along with Socrates and his reasoning, into the Barathrum. Oh! Clouds! all our troubles emanate from you, from you, to whom I entrusted myself, body and soul.

LEADER OF THE CHORUS: No, you alone are the cause, because you have pursued the path of evil.

STREPSIADES: Why did you not say so then, instead of egging on a poor ignorant old man?

LEADER OF THE CHORUS: We always act thus, when we see a man conceive a passion for what is evil; we strike him with some terrible disgrace, so that he may learn to fear the gods.

STREPSIADES: Alas! oh Clouds! that's hard indeed, but it's just! I ought not to have cheated my creditors....But come, my dear son, come with me to take vengeance on this wretched Chaerephon and on Socrates, who have deceived us both.

PHIDIPPIDES: I shall do nothing against our masters.

STREPSIADES: Oh show some reverence for ancestral Zeus!

PHIDIPPIDES: Mark him and his ancestral Zeus! What a fool you are! Does any such being as Zeus exist?

STREPSIADES: Why, assuredly.

PHIDIPPIDES: No, a thousand times no! The ruler of the world is the Whirlwind, that has unseated Zeus.

STREPSIADES: He has not dethroned him. I believed it, because of this whirligig here. Unhappy wretch that I am! I have taken a piece of clay to be a god.

PHIDIPPIDES: Very well! Keep your stupid nonsense for your own consumption. (He goes back into Strepsiades' house.)

STREPSIADES: Oh! what madness! I had lost my reason when I threw over the gods through Socrates' seductive phrases. (Addressing the statue of Hermes) Oh! good Hermes, do not destroy me in your wrath. Forgive me; their babbling had driven me crazy. Be my counselor. Shall I pursue them at law or shall I....? Order and I obey.-You are right, no law-suit; but up! let us burn down the home of those praters. Here, Xanthias, here! take a ladder, come forth and arm yourself with an axe; now mount upon the Thoughtery, demolish the roof, if you love your master, and may the house fall in upon them. Ho! bring me a blazing torch! There is more than one of them, arch-impostors as they are, on whom I am determined to have vengeance.

A DISCIPLE: (from within) Oh! oh!

STREPSIADES: Come, torch, do your duty! Burst into full flame!

DISCIPLE: What are you up to?

STREPSIADES: What am I up to? Why, I am entering upon a subtle argument with the beams of the house.

SECOND DISCIPLE: (from within) Hullo! hullo who is burning down our house?

STREPSIADES: The man whose cloak you have appropriated.

SECOND DISCIPLE: You are killing us!

STREPSIADES: That is just exactly what I hope, unless my axe plays me false, or I fall and break my neck.

SOCRATES: (appearing at the window) Hi! you fellow on the roof, what are you doing up there?

STREPSIADES: (mocking Socrates' manner) I am traversing the air and contemplating the sun.

SOCRATES: Ah! ah! woe is upon me! I am suffocating!

SECOND DISCIPLE: And I, alas, shall be burnt up!

STREPSIADES: Ah! you insulted the gods! You studied the face of the moon! Chase them, strike and beat them down! Forward! they have richly deserved their fate-above all, by reason of their blasphemies.

LEADER OF THE CHORUS: So let the Chorus file off the stage. Its part is played.

THE END

THE FROGS

CHARACTERS

XANTHIAS

servant of DIONYSUS

DIONYSUS

HERACLES

CHARON

AEACUS: :

A MAID SERVANT OF PERSEPHONE HOSTESS

keeper of cook-shop PLATHANE

her partner EURIPIDES:

AESCHYLUS:

PLUTO

CHORUS OF FROGS

THE FROGS

CHORUS OF BLESSED MYSTICS

The **SCENE** shows the house of Heracles   in the   background. There enter two travellers: Dionysus on foot, in his customary yellow robe and buskins but also with the club and lion's skin of Heracles, and his servant Xanthias on a donkey, carrying the luggage on a pole over his shoulder.

XANTHIAS: Shall I crack any of those old jokes, master,   At which the audience never fail to laugh?

DIONYSUS: Aye, what you will, except "I'm getting crushed": Fight shy of that: I'm sick of that already.

XANTHIAS: Nothing else smart?

DIONYSUS: Aye, save "my shoulder's aching."

XANTHIAS: Come now, that comical joke?

DIONYSUS: With all my heart. Only be careful not to shift your pole, And-

XANTHIAS: What?

DIONYSUS: And vow that you've a belly-ache.

XANTHIAS: May I not say I'm overburdened so That if none ease me, I must ease myself?

DIONYSUS: For mercy's sake, not till I'm going to vomit.

XANTHIAS: What! must I bear these burdens, and not make One of the jokes Ameipsias and Lycis And Phrynichus, in every play they write,   Put in the mouths of their burden-bearers?

DIONYSUS: Don't make them; no! I tell you when I see Their plays, and hear those jokes, I come away More than a twelvemonth older than I went.

117

XANTHIAS: O thrice unlucky neck of mine, which now Is getting crushed, yet must not crack its joke!

DIONYSUS: Now is not this fine pampered insolence When I myself, Dionysus, son of-Pipkin, Toil on afoot, and let this fellow ride, Taking no trouble, and no burden bearing?

XANTHIAS: What, don't I bear?

DIONYSUS: How can you when you're riding?

XANTHIAS: Why, I bear these.

DIONYSUS: How?

XANTHIAS: Most unwillingly.

DIONYSUS: Does not the donkey bear the load you're bearing?

XANTHIAS: Not what I bear myself: by Zeus, not he.

DIONYSUS: How can you bear, when you are borne yourself?

XANTHIAS: Don't know: but anyhow my shoulder's aching.

DIONYSUS: Then since you say the donkey helps you not, You lift him up and carry him in turn.

XANTHIAS: O hang it all! why didn't I fight at sea? You should have smarted bitterly for this.

DIONYSUS: Get down, you rascal; I've been trudging on Till now I've reached the portal, where I'm going First to turn in. Boy! Boy! I say there, Boy!

(Enter HERACLES: from house.)

118

HERACLES: Who banged the door? How like prancing Centaur He drove against it Mercy o' me, what's this?

DIONYSUS: Boy.

XANTHIAS: Yes.

DIONYSUS: Did you observe?

XANTHIAS: What?

DIONYSUS: How alarmed he is.

XANTHIAS: Aye truly, lest you've lost your wits.

HERACLES: O by Demeter, I can't choose but laugh. Biting my lips won't stop me. Ha! ha! ha!

DIONYSUS: Pray you, come hither, I have need of you.

HERACLES: I vow I can't help laughing, I can't help it. A lion's hide upon a yellow silk, A club and buskin! What's it all about? Where were you going?

DIONYSUS: I was serving lately Aboard the-Cleisthenes. More than a dozen of the enemy's ships.

HERACLES: You two?

DIONYSUS: We two.

HERACLES: And then I awoke, and lo!

DIONYSUS: There as, on deck, I'm reading to myself The Andromeda, a sudden pang of longing. Shoots through my heart, you can't conceive how keenly.

119

HERACLES: How big a pang?

DIONYSUS: A small one, Molon's size.

HERACLES: Caused by a woman?

DIONYSUS: No. Heracles   A boy?

DIONYSUS: No, no.

HERACLES: A man?

DIONYSUS: Ah! ah!

HERACLES: Was it for Cleisthenes?

DIONYSUS: Don't mock me, brother: on my life I am   In a bad way: such fierce desire consumes me.

HERACLES: Aye, little brother? how?

DIONYSUS: I can't describe it. But yet I'll tell you in a riddling way. Have you e'er felt a sudden lust for soup?

HERACLES: Soup! Zeus-a-mercy, yes, ten thousand times.

DIONYSUS: Is the thing clear, or must I speak again?

HERACLES: Not of the soup: I'm clear about the soup.

DIONYSUS: Well, just that sort of pang devours my heart   For lost Euripides.

HERACLES: A dead man too.

DIONYSUS: And no one shall persuade me not to go   After the man.

HERACLES: Do you mean below, to Hades?

DIONYSUS: And lower still, if there's a lower still.

HERACLES: What on earth for?

DIONYSUS: I want a genuine poet, "For some are not, and those that are, are bad."

HERACLES: What! does not Iophon live?

DIONYSUS: Well, he's the sole Good thing remaining, if even he is good. For even of that I'm not exactly certain.

HERACLES: If go you must, there's Sophocles-he comes Before Euripides- why not take him?

DIONYSUS: Not till I've tried if Iophon's coin rings true When he's alone, apart from Sophocles. Besides, Euripides , the crafty rogue, Will find a thousand shifts to get away, But he was easy here, is easy there.

HERACLES: But Agathon, where is he?

DIONYSUS: He has gone and left us. A genial poet, by his friends much missed.

HERACLES: Gone where?

DIONYSUS: To join the blessed in their banquets.

HERACLES: But what of Xenocles?

DIONYSUS: O he be hanged!

HERACLES: Pythangelus?

XANTHIAS: But never a word of me, Not though my shoulder's chafed so terribly.

HERACLES: But have you not a shoal of little songsters, Tragedians by the myriad, who can chatter A furlong faster than Euripides?

DIONYSUS: Those be mere vintage-leavings, jabberers, choirs Of swallow-broods, degraders of their art, Who get one chorus, and are seen no more, The Muses' love once gained. But O, my friend, Search where you will, you'll never find a true Creative genius, uttering startling things.

HERACLES: Creative? how do you mean? Who'll dare some novel venturesome conceit, "Air, Zeus's chamber," or "Time's foot," or this, "'Twas not my mind that swore: my tongue committed A little perjury on its own account."

HERACLES: You like that style?

DIONYSUS: Like it? I dote upon it.

HERACLES: I vow its ribald nonsense, and you know it.

DIONYSUS: "Rule not my mind": you've got a house to mind.

HERACLES: Really and truly though 'tis paltry stuff.

DIONYSUS: Teach me to dine!

XANTHIAS: But never a word of me.

DIONYSUS: But tell me truly-'twas for this I came Dressed up to mimic you-what friends received And entertained you when you went below To bring back Cerberus, in case I need them. And tell me too the havens, fountains, shops, Roads, resting-places, stews, refreshment-rooms, Towns, lodgings, hostesses, with whom were found The fewest bugs.

XANTHIAS: But never a word of me.

HERACLES: You are really game to go?

DIONYSUS: O drop that, can't you?   And tell me this: of all the roads you know   Which is the quickest way to get to Hades?   I want one not too warm, nor yet too cold.

HERACLES: Which shall I tell you first? which shall it be?   There's one by rope and bench: you launch away   And-hang yourself.

DIONYSUS: No thank you: that's too stifling.

HERACLES: Then there's a track, a short and beaten cut,   By pestle and mortar.

DIONYSUS: Hemlock, do you mean?

HERACLES: Just so.

DIONYSUS: No, that's too deathly cold a way;   You have hardly started ere your shins get numbed.

HERACLES: Well, would you like a steep and swift descent?

DIONYSUS: Aye, that's the style: my walking powers are small.

HERACLES: Go down to the Cerameicus.

DIONYSUS: And do what?

HERACLES: Climb to the tower's top pinnacle-

DIONYSUS: And then?

HERACLES: Observe the torch-race started, and when all The multitude is shouting "Let them go," Let yourself go.

DIONYSUS: Go! whither?

HERACLES: To the ground.

DIONYSUS: And lose, forsooth, two envelopes of brain. I'll not try that.

HERACLES: Which will you try?

DIONYSUS: The way You went yourself.

HERACLES: A parlous voyage that, For first you'll come to an enormous lake Of fathomless depth.

DIONYSUS: And how am I to cross?

HERACLES: An ancient mariner will row you over In a wee boat, so big. The fare's two obols.

DIONYSUS: Fie! The power two obols have, the whole world through! How came they thither!

HERACLES: Theseus took them down. And next you'll see great snakes and savage monsters In tens of thousands.

DIONYSUS: You needn't try to scare me, I'm going to go.

HERACLES: Then weltering seas of filth And ever-rippling dung: and plunged therein, Whoso has wronged the stranger here on earth, Or robbed his boylove of the promised pay, Or swinged his mother, or profanely smitten His father's check, or sworn an oath forsworn, Or copied out a speech of Morsimus.

DIONYSUS: There too, perdie, should he be plunged, whoe'er Has danced the sword-dance of Cinesias.

HERACLES: And next the breath of flutes will float around you,   And glorious sunshine, such as ours, you'll see,   And myrtle groves, and happy bands who clap   Their hands in triumph, men and women too.

DIONYSUS: And who are they?

HERACLES: The happy mystic bands,

XANTHIAS: And I'm the donkey in the mystery show.   But I'll not stand it, not one instant longer.

HERACLES: Who'll tell you everything you want to know.   You'll find them dwelling close beside the road   You are going to travel, just at Pluto's gate.   And fare thee well, my brother.

DIONYSUS: And to you Good cheer. (Exit HERACLES: .)   Now sirrah, pick you up the traps.

XANTHIAS: Before I've put them down?

DIONYSUS: And quickly too.

XANTHIAS: No, prithee, no: but hire a body, one   They're carrying out, on purpose for the trip.

DIONYSUS: If I can't find one?

XANTHIAS: Then I'll take them.

DIONYSUS: Good.   And see they are carrying out a body now.   Here a corpse, wrapped in its grave-clothes,   and lying on a bier, is carried across the stage. Hallo! you there, you deadman, are you willing   To carry down our little traps to Hades?

CORPSE: What are they?

125

DIONYSUS: These.

CORPSE: Two drachmas for the job?

DIONYSUS: Nay, that's too much.

CORPSE: Out of the pathway, you!

DIONYSUS: Beshrew thee, stop: may-be we'll strike a bargain.

CORPSE: Pay me two drachmas, or it's no use talking.

DIONYSUS: One and a half.

CORPSE: I'd liefer live again I.

XANTHIAS: How absolute the knave is! He be hanged! I'll go myself.

DIONYSUS: You're the right sort, my man. Now to the ferry.

(Enter CHARON.)

CHARON: Yoh, up! lay her to.

XANTHIAS: Whatever's that?

DIONYSUS: Why, that's the lake, by Zeus, Whereof he spake, and yon's the ferry-boat.

XANTHIAS: Poseidon, yes, and that old fellow's Charon.

DIONYSUS: Charon! O welcome, Charon! welcome, Charon!

CHARON: Who's for the Rest from every pain and ill? Who's for the Lethe's plain? the Donkey-shearings? Who's for Cerberia? Taenarum? or the Ravens?

DIONYSUS: I.

CHARON: Hurry in.

DIONYSUS: But where are you going really? In truth to the Ravens?

CHARON: Aye, for your behoof. Step in.

DIONYSUS: (to XANTHIAS) Now, lad.

CHARON: A slave? I take no slave, Unless he has fought for his bodyrights at sea.

XANTHIAS: I couldn't go. I'd got the eye-disease.

CHARON: Then fetch a circuit round about the lake.

XANTHIAS: Where must I wait?

CHARON: Beside the Withering stone, Hard by the Rest.

DIONYSUS: You understand?

XANTHIAS: Too well. O, what ill omen crossed me as I started! Exit.

CHARON: (to **DIONYSUS**) Sit to the oar. (calling) Who else for the boat? Be quick. (to **DIONYSUS**) Hi! what are you doing?

DIONYSUS: What am I doing? Sitting On to the oar. You told me to, yourself

CHARON: Now sit you there, you little Potgut.

DIONYSUS: Now stretch your arms full length before you.

CHARON: Come, don't keep fooling; plant your feet, Pull with a will.

127

DIONYSUS: Why, how am I to pull? I'm not an oarsman, seaman, Salaminian. I can't.

CHARON: You can. Just dip your oar in once, You'll hear the loveliest timing songs.

DIONYSUS: What from?

CHARON: Frog-swans, most wonderful.

DIONYSUS: Then give the word.

CHARON: Heave ahoy! heave ahoy I.

FROGS: (off stage) Brekekekex, ko-ax, ko-ax, Brekekekex, ko-ax, ko-ax! We children of the fountain and the lake Let us wake Our full choir-shout, as the flutes are ringing out, Our symphony of clear-voiced song. The song we used to love in the Marshland up above, In praise of Dionysus to produce, Of Nysaean Dionysus, son of Zeus, When the revel-tipsy throng, all crapulous and gay, To our precinct reeled along on the holy Pitcher day, Brekekekex, ko-ax, ko-ax.

DIONYSUS: O, dear! O, dear! now I declare I've got a bump upon my rump,

FROGS: Brekekekex, ko-ax, ko-ax.

DIONYSUS: But you, perchance, don't care.

FROGS: Brekekekex, ko-ax, ko-ax.

DIONYSUS: Hang you, and your ko-axing tool There's nothing but ko-ax with you.

FROGS: That is right, Mr. Busybody, right! For the Muses of the lyre love us well; And hornfoot Pan who plays on the pipe his jocund lays; And Apollo, Harper bright, in our chorus takes delight; For the strong reed's sake which I

128

grow within my lake To be girdled in his lyre's deep shell. Brekekekex, ko-ax, ko-ax.

DIONYSUS: My hands are blistered very sore; My stern below is sweltering so, 'Twill soon, I know, upturn and roar Brekekekex, ko-ax, ko-ax. O tuneful race, O pray give o'er, O sing no more.

FROGS: Ah, no! ah, no! Loud and louder our chant must flow. Sing if ever ye sang of yore, When in sunny and glorious days Through the rushes and marsh-flags springing On we swept, in the joy of singing Myriad-diving roundelays. Or when fleeing the storm, we went Down to the depths, and our choral song Wildly raised to a loud and long Bubble-bursting accompaniment.

FROGS: and **DIONYSUS**:   Brekekekex, ko-ax, ko-ax.

DIONYSUS: This timing song I take from you.

FROGS: That's a dreadful thing to do. DIONYSUS: Much more dreadful, if I row Till I burst myself, I trow.

FROGS: and **DIONYSUS**:   Brekekekex, ko-ax, ko-ax.

DIONYSUS: Go, hang yourselves; for what care I?

FROGS: All the same we'll shout and cry, Stretching all our throats with song, Shouting, crying, all day long,

FROGS: and **DIONYSUS**:   Brekekekex, ko-ax, ko-ax.

DIONYSUS: In this you'll never, never win.

FROGS: This you shall not beat us in.

DIONYSUS: No, nor ye prevail o'er me. Never! never! I'll my song, Shout, if need be, all day Yong, Until I've learned to master your ko-ax. Brekekekex, ko-ax, ko-ax. I thought I'd put
a stop to your ko-ax.

CHARON: Stop! Easy! Take the oar and push her to. Now pay your fare and go.

DIONYSUS: Here' tis: two obols. Xanthias! where's Xanthias ? Is it Xanthias there?

XANTHIAS: (off stage) Hoi, hoi!

DIONYSUS: Come hither.

XANTHIAS: (Entering) Glad to meet you, master.

DIONYSUS: What have you there?

XANTHIAS: Nothing but filth and darkness.

DIONYSUS: But tell me, did you see the PARRICIDE: s And perjured folk he mentioned?

XANTHIAS: Didn't you?

DIONYSUS: Poseidon, yes. Why look! (pointing to the audience) I see them now. What's the next step?

XANTHIAS: We'd best be moving on. This is the spot where

HERACLES: declared Those savage monsters dwell.

DIONYSUS: O hang the fellow. That's all his bluff: he

thought to scare me off, The jealous dog, knowing my plucky ways. There's no such swaggerer lives as Heracles. Why, I'd like nothing better than to achieve Some bold adventure, worthy of our trip.

XANTHIAS: I know you would. Hallo! I hear a noise.

DIONYSUS: Where? what?

XANTHIAS: Behind us, there.

DIONYSUS: Get you behind.

XANTHIAS: No, it's in front.

DIONYSUS: Get you in front directly.

XANTHIAS: And now I see the most ferocious monster.

DIONYSUS: O, what's it like?

XANTHIAS: Like everything by turns. Now it's a bull: now it's a mule: and now The loveliest girl.

DIONYSUS: O, where? I'll go and meet her.

XANTHIAS: It's ceased to be a girl: it's a dog now.

DIONYSUS: It is Empusa!

XANTHIAS: Well, its face is all Ablaze with fire.

DIONYSUS: Has it a copper leg?

XANTHIAS: A copper leg? yes, one; and one of cow dung.

DIONYSUS: O, whither shall I flee?

131

XANTHIAS: O, whither I?

DIONYSUS: My PRIEST: , protect me, and we'll sup together.

XANTHIAS: King Heracles, we're done for.

DIONYSUS: O, forbear, Good fellow, call me anything but that.

XANTHIAS: Well then, Dionysus.

DIONYSUS: O, that's worse again,

XANTHIAS: (to the SPECTRE) Aye, go thy way. O master, here, come here.

DIONYSUS: O, what's up now?

XANTHIAS: Take courage; all's serene. And, like Hegelochus, we now may say "Out of the storm there comes a new wether." Empusa's gone.

DIONYSUS: Swear it.

XANTHIAS: By Zeus she is.

DIONYSUS: Swear it again.

XANTHIAS: By Zeus.

DIONYSUS: Again.

XANTHIAS: By Zeus. O dear, O dear, how pale I grew to see her, But he, from fright has yellowed me all over.

DIONYSUS: Ah me, whence fall these evils on my head? on Who is the god to blame for my destruction? Air, Zeus's chamber, or the Foot of Time? (A flute is played behind the scenes.)

XANTHIAS: What's the matter?

DIONYSUS: The breath of flutes.

XANTHIAS: Aye, and a whiff of torches Breathed o'er me too; a very mystic whiff.

DIONYSUS: Then crouch we down, and mark what's going on.

CHORUS: (in the distance) O Iacchus! O Iacchus! O Iacchus!

XANTHIAS: I have it, master: 'tis those blessed Mystics, Of whom he told us, sporting hereabouts. They sing the Iacchus which Diagoras made.

DIONYSUS: I think so too: we had better both keep quiet And so find out exactly what it is. Enter Chorus, who had chanted the songs of the Frogs, as initiates.

CHORUS: O Iacchus! power excelling, here in stately temples dwelling. O Iacchus! O Iacchus! Come to tread this verdant level, Come to dance in mystic revel, Come whilst round thy forehead hurtles Many a wreath of fruitful myrtles, Come with wild and saucy paces Mingling in our joyous dance, Pure and holy, which embraces all the charms of all the Graces, When the mystic choirs advance.

XANTHIAS: Holy and sacred queen, Demeter's daughter, O, what a jolly whiff of pork breathed o'er me!

DIONYSUS: Hist! and perchance you'll get some tripe yourself.

CHORUS: Come, arise, from sleep awaking, come the fiery torches shaking, O Iacchus! O Iacchus! Morning Star that shinest nightly. Lo, the mead is blazing brightly, Age forgets its years and sadness, Aged knees curvet for gladness, Lift thy flashing torches o'er us, Marshal all thy blameless train, Lead, O lead the way before us; lead the lovely youthful chorus to the marshy
133

flowery plain. All evil thoughts and profane be still: far hence, far hence from our choirs depart, Who knows not well what the Mystics tell, or is not holy and pure of heart; Who ne'er has the noble revelry learned, or danced the dance of the Muses high; or shared in the Bacchic rites which old bull-eating Cratinus's words supply; Who vulgar coarse buffoonery loves, though all untimely the they make; Or lives not easy and kind with all, or kindling faction forbears to slake, But fans the fire, from a base desire some pitiful gain for himself to reap; Or takes, in office, his gifts and bribes, while the city is tossed on the stormy deep; Who fort or fleet to the foe betrays; or, a vile Thorycion, ships away Forbidden stores from Aegina's shores, to Epidaurus across the Bay Transmitting oar-pads and sails and tar, that curst collector of five per cents; The knave who tries to procure supplies for the use of the enemy's armaments; The Cyclian singer who dares befoul the Lady Hecate's wayside shrine; The public speaker who once lampooned in our Bacchic feasts would, with heart malign, Keep nibbling away the Comedians' pay;- to these I utter my warning cry, I charge them once, I charge them twice, I charge them thrice, that they draw not nigh To the sacred dance of the Mystic choir. But ye, my comrades, awake the song, The night-long revels of joy and mirth which ever of right to our feast belong. Advance, true hearts, advance! On to the gladsome bowers, On to the sward, with flowers Embosomed bright! March on with jest, and jeer, and dance, Full well ye've supped to-night. March, chanting loud your lays, Your hearts and voices raising, The Saviour goddess praising Who vows she'll still Our city save to endless days, Whate'er Thorycion's will. Break off the measure, and change the time; and now with chanting and hymns adorn Demeter, goddess mighty and high, the harvest-queen, the giver of corn. O Lady, over our rites presiding, Preserve and succour thy choral throng, And grant us all, in thy help confiding, To dance and revel the whole day long; And much in earnest, and much in jest, Worthy thy feast, may we speak therein. And when we have bantered and laughed our best, The victor's wreath be it ours to win. Call we now the youthful god, call him hither without delay, Him who travels amongst his chorus, dancing along on the Sacred Way. O, come with the joy of thy festival song, O, come to the goddess, O, mix with our throng Untired, though the journey be never so long. O Lord of the frolic and dance, Iacchus, beside me advance! For fun, and for cheapness, our dress thou hast rent, Through thee we may dance to the top of our bent, Reviling, and jeering, and none will resent. O Lord of the frolic and dance, Iacchus, beside me advance! A sweet pretty girl I observed in the show, Her robe had been torn in the scuffle, and lo, There peeped through the tatters a bosom of snow. O Lord of the frolic and dance, Iacchus, beside me advance!

DIONYSUS: Wouldn't I like to follow on, and try A little sport and dancing?

XANTHIAS: Wouldn't I?

CHORUS: Shall we all a merry joke At Archedemus poke, Who has not cut his guildsmen yet, though seven years old; Yet up among the dead He is demagogue and head And contrives the topmost place of the rascaldom to hold? And Cleisthenes, they say, Is among the tombs all day, Bewailing for his lover with a lamentable whine. And Callias, I'm told, Has become a sailor bold, And casts a lion's hide o'er his members feminine.

DIONYSUS: Can any of you tell Where Pluto here may dwell, For we, sirs, are two strangers who were never here before?

CHORUS: O, then no further stray, Nor again inquire the way, For know that ye have journeyed to his very entrance-door.

DIONYSUS: Take up the wraps, my lad.

XANTHIAS: Now is not this too bad? Like "Zeus's Corinth," he "the wraps" keeps saying o'er and o'er.

CHORUS: Now wheel your sacred dances through the glade with flowers bedight, All ye who are partakers of the holy festal rite; And I will with the women and the holy maidens go Where they keep the nightly vigil, an auspicious light to show. Now haste we to the roses, And the meadows full of posies, Now haste we to the meadows In our own old way, In choral dances blending, In dances never ending, Which only for the holy The Destinies array. O, happy mystic chorus, The blessed sunshine o'er us On us alone is smiling, In its soft sweet light: On us who strove forever With holy, pure endeavour, Alike by friend and stranger To guide our steps aright.

135

DIONYSUS: What's the right way to knock? I wonder how The natives here are wont to knock at doors.

XANTHIAS: No dawdling: taste the door. You've got, remember, The lion-hide and pride of Heracles.

DIONYSUS: (knocking) Boy! boy! The door opens. Aeacus appears.

AEACUS: Who's there?

DIONYSUS: I, Heracles the strong!

AEACUS: O, you most shameless desperate ruffian, you O, villain, villain, arrant vilest villain! Who seized our Cerberus by the throat, and fled, And ran, and rushed, and bolted, haling of The dog, my charge! But now I've got thee fast. So close the Styx's inky-hearted rock, The blood-bedabbled peak of Acheron Shall hem thee in: the hell-hounds of Cocytus Prowl round thee; whilst the hundred-headed Asp Shall rive thy heart-strings: the Tartesian Lamprey Prey on thy lungs: and those Tithrasian Gorgons Mangle and tear thy kidneys, mauling them, Entrails and all, into one bloody mash. I'll speed a running foot to fetch them hither. Exit Aeacus.

XANTHIAS: Hallo! what now?

DIONYSUS: I've done it: call the god.

XANTHIAS: Get up, you laughing-stock; get up directly, Before you're seen.

DIONYSUS: What, I get up? I'm fainting. Please dab a sponge of water on my heart.

XANTHIAS: Here! Dab it on.

DIONYSUS: Where is it?

XANTHIAS: Ye golden gods, Lies your heart there?

DIONYSUS: It got so terrified It fluttered down into my stomach's pit.

XANTHIAS: Cowardliest of gods and men!

DIONYSUS: The cowardliest? I? What I, who asked you for a sponge, a thing A coward never would have done!

XANTHIAS: What then?

DIONYSUS: A coward would have lain there wallowing; But I stood up, and wiped myself withal.

XANTHIAS: Poseidon! quite heroic.

DIONYSUS: 'Deed I think so. But weren't you frightened at those dreadful threats And shoutings?

XANTHIAS: Frightened? Not a bit. I cared not.

DIONYSUS: Come then, if you're so very brave a man, Will you be I, and take the hero's club And lion's skin, since you're so monstrous plucky? And I'll be now the slave, and bear the luggage.

XANTHIAS: Hand them across. I cannot choose but take them. And now observe the Xanthio-Heracles. If I'm a coward and a sneak like you.

DIONYSUS: Nay, you're the rogue from Melite's own self. And I'll pick up and carry on the traps. Enter a maid-servant of Persephone, from the door.

MAID: O welcome, Heracles! come in, sweetheart. My Lidy, when they told her, set to work, baked mighty loaves, boiled two or three tureens of lentil soup, roasted a prime ox whole, made rolls and honey-cakes. So come along.

XANTHIAS: (declining) You are too kind.

MAID: I will not let you go. I will not let you! Why, she's stewing slices Of juicy bird's-flesh, and she's making comfits, And tempering down her richest wine. Come, dear, Come along in.

XANTHIAS: (still declining) Pray thank her.

MAID: O you're jesting, I shall not let you off: there's such a lovely Flute-girl all ready, and we've two or three Dancing-girls also.

XANTHIAS: Eh! what! Dancing-girls?

MAID: Young budding virgins, freshly tired and trimmed. Come, dear, come in. The cook was dishing up The cutlets, and they are bringing in the tables.

XANTHIAS: Then go you in, and tell those dancing-girls Of whom you spake, I'm coming in Myself. Exit maid. Pick up the traps, my lad, and follow me.

DIONYSUS: Hi! stop! you're not in earnest, just because I dressed you up, in fun, as Heracles? Come, don't keep fooling, Xanthias, but lift And carry in the traps yourself You are never going to strip me of these togs you gave me!

DIONYSUS: Going to? No, I'm doing it now. Off with that lion-skin.

XANTHIAS: Bear witness all, The gods shall judge between us.

DIONYSUS: Gods, indeed! Why, how could you (the vain and foolish thought I) A slave, a mortal, act Alemena's son?

XANTHIAS: All right then, take them; maybe, if God will, You'll soon require my services again.

CHORUS: This is the part of a dexterous clever Man with his wits about him ever, One who has travelled the world to see; Always to shift, and to keep through all Close to the sunny side of the wall; Not like a pictured block to be, Standing always in one position; Nay but to veer, with expedition, And ever to

138

catch the favouring breeze, This is the part of a shrewd tactician, This is to be a-Theramenes!

DIONYSUS: Truly an exquisite joke 'twould be, Him with a dancing-girl to see, Lolling at ease on Milesian rugs; Me, like a slave, beside him standing, Aught that he wants to his lordship handing; Then as the damsel fair he hugs, Seeing me all on fire to embrace her, He would perchance (for there's no man baser), Turning him round like a lazy lout, Straight on my mouth deliver a facer, Knocking my ivory choirmen out.

(Enter HOSTESS and PLATHANE.)

HOSTESS: O Plathane! Plathane! that naughty man, That's he who got into our tavern once, And ate up sixteen loaves.

PLATHANE: O, so he is! The very man.

XANTHIAS: Bad luck for somebody!

HOSTESS: O and, besides, those twenty bits of stew, Half-obol pieces.

XANTHIAS: Somebody's going to catch it!

HOSTESS: That garlic too.

DIONYSUS: Woman, you're talking nonsense. You don't know what you're saying.

HOSTESS: O, you thought I shouldn't know you with your buskins on! Ah, and I've not yet mentioned all that fish, No, nor the new-made cheese: he gulped it down, Baskets and all, unlucky that we were. And when I just alluded to the price, He looked so fierce, and bellowed like a bull.

XANTHIAS: Yes, that's his way: that's what he always does.

HOSTESS: O, and he drew his sword, and seemed quite mad.

PLATHANE: O, that he did. HOSTESS And terrified us so We sprang up to the cockloft, she and I. Then out he hurled, decamping with the rugs.

XANTHIAS: That's his way too; something must be done.

HOSTESS: Quick, run and call my patron Cleon here

PLATHANE: O, if you meet him, call Hyperbolus! We'll pay you out to-day.

HOSTESS: O filthy throat, O how I'd like to take a stone, and hack Those grinders out with which you chawed my wares.

PLATHANE: I'd like to pitch you in the deadman's pit.

HOSTESS: I'd like to get a reaping-hook and scoop That gullet out with which you gorged my tripe. But I'll to Cleon: he'll soon serve his writs; He'll twist it out of you to-day, he will.

(Exit HOSTESS and PLATHANE.)

DIONYSUS: Perdition seize me, if I don't love Xanthias.

XANTHIAS: Aye, aye, I know your drift: stop, stop that talking I won't be Heracles.

DIONYSUS: O, don't say so, Dear, darling Xanthias.

XANTHIAS: Why, how can I, A slave, a mortal, act Alemena's son!

DIONYSUS: Aye, aye, I know you are vexed, and I deserve And if you pummel me, I won't complain. But if I strip you of these togs again, Perdition seize myself, my wife, my children, And, most of all, that blear-eyed Archedemus.

XANTHIAS: That oath contents me: on those terms I take them.

140

CHORUS: Now that at last you appear once more, Wearing the garb that at first you wore, Wielding the club and the tawny skin, Now it is yours to be up and doing, Glaring like mad, and your youth renewing, Mindful of him whose guise you are in. If, when caught in a bit of a scrape, you Suffer a word of alarm to escape you, Showing yourself but a feckless knave, Then will your master at once undrape you, Then you'll again be the toiling slave.

XANTHIAS: There, I admit, you have given to me Capital hint, and the like idea, Friends, had occurred to myself before. Truly if anything good befell He would be wanting, I know full well, Wanting to take to the togs once more. Nevertheless, while in these I'm vested, Ne'er shall you find me craven-crested, No, for a dittany look I'll wear, Aye and methinks it will soon be tested, Hark! how the portals are rustling there.

Re-enter AEACUS: with assistants.

AEACUS: Seize the dog-stealer, bind him, pinion him, Drag him to justice

DIONYSUS: Somebody's going to catch it.

XANTHIAS: (striking out) Hands off! away! stand back!

AEACUS: Eh? You're for fighting. Ho! Ditylas, Sceblyas, and Pardocas, Come hither, quick; fight me this sturdy knave.

DIONYSUS: Now isn't it a shame the man should strike And he a thief besides?

AEACUS: A monstrous shame!

DIONYSUS: A regular burning shame!

XANTHIAS: By the Lord Zeus, If ever I was here before, if ever I stole one hair's-worth from you, let me die! And now I'll make you a right noble offer,

141

Arrest my lad: torture him as you will, And if you find I'm guilty, take and kill me.

AEACUS: Torture him, how?

XANTHIAS: In any mode you please. Pile bricks upon him: stuff his nose with acid: Flay, rack him, hoist him; flog him with a scourge Of prickly bristles: only not with this, A soft-leaved onion, or a tender leek.

AEACUS: A fair proposal. If I strike too hard And maim the boy, I'll make you compensation.

XANTHIAS: I shan't require it. Take him out and flog him.

AEACUS: Nay, but I'll do it here before your eyes. Now then, put down the traps, and mind you speak The truth, young fellow.

DIONYSUS: (in agony) Man' don't torture me! I am a god. You'll blame yourself hereafter If you touch me.

AEACUS: Hillo! What's that you are saying?

DIONYSUS: I say I'm Bacchus, son of Zeus, a god, And he's the slave.

AEACUS: You hear him?

XANTHIAS: Hear him? Yes. All the more reason you should flog him well. For if he is a god, he won't perceive it.

DIONYSUS: Well, but you say that you're a god yourself. So why not you be flogged as well as I?

XANTHIAS: A fair proposal. And be this the test, Whichever of us two you first behold Flinching or crying out-he's not the god.

142

AEACUS: Upon my word you're quite the gentleman, You're all for right and justice. Strip then, both.

XANTHIAS: How can you test us fairly?

AEACUS: Easily. I'll give you blow for blow.

XANTHIAS: A good idea. We're ready now! (Aeacus: strikes him) see if you catch me flinching.

AEACUS: I struck you.

XANTHIAS: (incredulously) No!

AEACUS: Well, it seems "no" indeed. Now then I'll strike the other.

(Strikes DIONYSUS.)

DIONYSUS: Tell me when?

AEACUS: I struck you.

DIONYSUS: Struck me? Then why didn't I sneeze?

AEACUS: Don't know, I'm sure. I'll try the other again.

XANTHIAS: And quickly too. Good gracious!

AEACUS: Why "good gracious"? Not hurt you, did I?

XANTHIAS: No, I merely thought of The Diomeian feast of Heracles.

AEACUS: A holy man! 'Tis now the other's turn.

DIONYSUS: Hi! Hi!

143

AEACUS: Hallo!

DIONYSUS: Look at those horsemen, look!

AEACUS: But why these tears?

DIONYSUS: There's such a smell of onions.

AEACUS: Then you don't mind it?

DIONYSUS: (cheerfully) Mind it? Not a bit.

AEACUS: Well, I must go to the other one again.

XANTHIAS: O! O!

AEACUS: Hallo!

XANTHIAS: Do pray pull out this thorn.

AEACUS: What does it mean? 'Tis this one's turn again.

DIONYSUS: (shrieking) Apollo! Lord! (calmly) of Delos and of Pytho.

XANTHIAS: He flinched! You heard him?

DIONYSUS: Not at all; a jolly Verse of Hipponax flashed across my mind.

XANTHIAS: You don't half do it: cut his flanks to pieces.

AEACUS: By Zeus, well thought on. Turn your belly here.

DIONYSUS: (screaming) Poseidon!

XANTHIAS: There! he's flinching.

DIONYSUS: (singing) who dost reign Amongst the Aegean peaks and creeks And oer the deep blue main.

AEACUS: No, by Demeter, still I can't find out Which is the god, but come ye both indoors; My lord himself and Persephassa there, Being gods themselves, will soon find out the truth.

DIONYSUS: Right! right! I only wish you had thought of that Before you gave me those tremendous whacks.

Exit DIONYSUS, XANTHIAS, AEACUS, and attendants.

CHORUS: Come, Muse, to our Mystical Chorus, O come to the joy of my song, O see on the benches before us that countless and wonderful throng, Where wits by the thousand abide, with more than a Cleophon's pride- On the lips of that foreigner base, of Athens the bane and disgrace, There is shrieking, his kinsman by race, The garrulous swallow of Thrace; From that perch of exotic descent, Rejoicing her sorrow to vent, She pours to her spirit's content, a nightingale's woful lament, That e'en though the voting be equal, his ruin will soon be the sequel. Well it suits the holy CHORUS: evermore with counsel wise To exhort and teach the city; this we therefore now advise- End the townsmen's apprehensions; equalize the rights of all; If by Phrynichus's wrestlings some perchance sustained a fall, Yet to these 'tis surely open, having put away their sin, For their slips and vacillations pardon at your hands to win. Give your brethren back their franchise. Sin and shame it were that slaves, Who have once with stern devotion fought your battle on the waves, Should be straightway lords and masters, yea Plataeans fully blown- Not that this deserves our censure; there I praise you; there alone Has the city, in her anguish, policy and wisdom shown- Nay but these, of old accustomed on our ships to fight and win, (They, their fathers too before them), these our very kith and kin, You should likewise, when they ask you, pardon for their single sin. O by nature best and wisest, O relax your jealous ire, Let us all the world as kinsfolk and as citizens acquire, All who on our ships will battle well and bravely by our side. If we cocker up our city, narrowing her with senseless pride, Now when she is rocked and reeling in the cradles of the sea, Here again will after ages deem we acted
145

brainlessly. And O if I'm able to scan the habits and life of a man Who shall rue his iniquities soon! not long shall that little baboon, That Cleigenes shifty and small, the wickedest bathman of all Who are lords of the earth-which is brought from the isle of Cimolus, and wrought With nitre and lye into soap- Not long shall he vex us, I hope. And this the unlucky one knows, Yet ventures a peace to oppose, And being addicted to blows he carries a stick as he goes, Lest while he is tipsy and reeling, some robber his cloak should be stealing. Often has it crossed my fancy, that the city loves to deal With the very best and noblest members of her commonweal, just as with our ancient coinage, and the newly-minted gold. Yea for these, our sterling pieces, all of pure Athenian mould, All of perfect die and metal, all the fairest of the fair, All of workmanship unequalled, proved and valued everywhere Both amongst our own Hellenes and Barbarians far away, These we use not: but the worthles pinchbeck coins of yesterday, Vilest die and basest metal, now we always use instead. Even so, our sterling townsmen, nobly born and nobly bred, Men of worth and rank and mettle, men of honourable fame, Trained in every liberal science, choral dance and manly game, These we treat with scorn and insult, but the strangers newliest come, Worthless sons of worthless fathers, pinchbeck townsmen, yellowy scum, Whom in earlier days the city hardly would have stooped to use Even for her scapegoat victims, these for every task we choose. O unwise and foolish people, yet to mend your ways begin; Use again the good and useful: so hereafter, if ye win 'Twill be due to this your wisdom: if ye fall, at least 'twill be Not a fall that brings dishonour, falling from a worthy tree.

Enter AEACUS, XANTHIAS and two attendants.

AEACUS: By Zeus the Saviour, quite the gentleman Your master is.

XANTHIAS: Gentleman? I believe you. He's all for wine and women, is my master.

AEACUS: But not to have flogged you, when the truth came out That you, the slave, were passing off as master!

XANTHIAS: He'd get the worst of that.

AEACUS: Bravo! that's spoken Like a true slave: that's what I love myself.

XANTHIAS: You love it, do you?

AEACUS: Love it? I'm entranced When I can curse my lord behind his back.

XANTHIAS: How about grumbling, when you have felt the stick, And scurry out of doors?

AEACUS: That's jolly too.

XANTHIAS: How about prying?

AEACUS: That beats everything,

XANTHIAS: Great Kin-god Zeus! And what of overhearing Your master's secrets?

AEACUS: What? I'm mad with joy.

XANTHIAS: And blabbing them abroad?

AEACUS: O heaven and earth! When I do that, I can't contain myself.

XANTHIAS: Phoebus Apollo! clap your hand in mine, Kiss and be kissed: and prithee tell me this, Tell me by Zeus, our rascaldom's own god, What's all that noise within? What means this hubbub And row?

AEACUS: That's Aeschylus and Euripides.

XANTHIAS: Eh?

AEACUS: Wonderful, wonderful things are going on. The dead are rioting, taking different sides.

XANTHIAS: Why, what's the matter?

AEACUS: There's a custom here With all the crafts, the good and noble crafts, That the chief master of art in each Shall have his dinner in the assembly hall, And sit by Pluto's side.

XANTHIAS: I understand.

AEACUS: Until another comes, more wise than he In the same art: then must the first give way.

XANTHIAS: And how has this disturbed our Aeschylus?

AEACUS: 'Twas he that occupied the tragic chair, As, in his craft, the noblest.

XANTHIAS: Who does now?

AEACUS: But when Euripides came down, he kept Flourishing off before the highwaymen, Thieves, burglars, Parricides-these form our mob In Hades-till with listening to his twists And turns, and pleas and counterpleas, they went Mad on the man, and hailed him first and wisest: Elate with this, he claimed the tragic chair where Aeschylus was seated.

XANTHIAS: Wasn't he pelted?

AEACUS: Not he: the populace clamoured out to try Which of the twain was wiser in his art.

XANTHIAS: You mean the rascals?

AEACUS: Aye, as high as heaven!

XANTHIAS: But were there none to side with Aeschylus?

AEACUS: Scanty and sparse the good, (regards the   audience) the same as here.

148

XANTHIAS: And what does Pluto now propose to do?

AEACUS: He means to hold a tournament, and bring Their tragedies to the proof.

XANTHIAS: But Sophocles, How came not he to claim the tragic chair?

AEACUS: Claim it? Not he! When he came down, he kissed With reverence Aeschylus, and clasped his hand, And yielded willingly the chair to him. But now he's going, says Cleidemides, To sit third-man: and then if Aeschylus win, He'll stay content: if not, for his art's sake, He'll fight to the death against Euripides.

XANTHIAS: Will it come off?

AEACUS: O yes, by Zeus, directly. And then, I hear, will wonderful things be done, The art poetic will be weighed in scales.

XANTHIAS: What I weigh out tragedy, like butcher's meat?

AEACUS: Levels they'll bring, and measuring-tapes for words, And moulded oblongs,

XANTHIAS: Is it bricks they are making?

AEACUS: Wedges and compasses: for Euripides vows that he'll test the dramas, word by word.

XANTHIAS: Aeschylus chafes at this, I fancy.

AEACUS: Well, He lowered his brows, upglaring like a bull.

XANTHIAS: And who's to be the judge?

AEACUS: There came the rub. Skilled men were hard to find: for with the Athenians Aeschylus, somehow, did not hit it off,

XANTHIAS: Too many burglars, I expect, he thought.

AEACUS: And all the rest, he said, were trash and nonsense To judge poetic wits. So then at last They chose your lord, an expert in the art. But we go in for when our lords are bent On urgent business, that means blows for us.

CHORUS: O surely with terrible wrath will the thunder-voiced monarch be filled, When he sees his opponent beside him, the tonguester, the artifice-skilled, Stand, whetting his tusks for the fight! O surely, his eyes rolling-fell Will with terrible madness be fraught I O then will be charging of plume-waving words with their wild-floating mane, And then will be whirling of splinters, and phrases smoothed down with the plane, When the man would the grand-stepping maxims, the language gigantic, repel Of the hero-creator of thought. There will his shaggy-born crest upbristle for anger and woe, Horribly frowning and growling, his fury will launch at the foe Huge-clamped masses of words, with exertion Titanic up-tearing Great ship-timber planks for the fray. But here will the tongue be at work, uncoiling, word-testing, refining, Sophist-creator of phrases, dissecting, detracting, maligning, Shaking the envious bits, and with subtle analysis paring The lung's large labour away. Here apparently there is a complete change of scene, to the Hall of Pluto, with himself sitting on his throne, and Dionysus, Aeschylus, and the foreground.

EURIPIDES: Don't talk to me; I won't give up the chair, I say I am better in the art than he.

DIONYSUS: You hear him, Aeschylus why don't you speak?

EURIPIDES: He'll do the grand at first, the juggling trick He used to play in all his tragedies.

DIONYSUS: Come, my fine fellow, pray don't talk to big.

EURIPIDES: I know the man, I've scanned him through and through, A savage-creating stubborn-pulling fellow, Uncurbed, unfettered, uncontrolled of speech, Unperiphrastic, bombastiloquent.

150

AESCHYLUS: Hah! sayest thou so, child of the garden quean And this to me, thou chattery-babble-collector, Thou pauper-creating rags-and-patches-stitcher? Thou shalt abye it dearly!

DIONYSUS: Pray, be still; Nor heat thy soul to fury, Aeschylus.

AESCHYLUS: Not till I've made you see the sort of man This cripple-maker is who crows so loudly.

DIONYSUS: Bring out a ewe, a black-fleeced ewe, my boys: Here's a typhoon about to burst upon us.

AESCHYLUS: Thou picker-up of Cretan monodies, Foisting thy tales of incest on the stage-

DIONYSUS: Forbear, forbear, most honoured Aeschylus; And you, my poor Euripides, begone If you are wise, out of this pitiless hail, Lest with some heady word he crack your scull And batter out your brain-less Telephus. And not with passion, Aeschylus, but calmly Test and be tested. 'Tis not meet for poets To scold each other, like two baking-girls. But you go roaring like an oak on fire.

EURIPIDES: I'm ready, I don't draw back one bit. I'll lash or, if he will, let him lash first The talk, the lays, the sinews of a play: Aye and my Peleus, aye and Aeolus. And Meleager, aye and Telephus.

DIONYSUS: And what do you propose? Speak, Aeschylus.

AESCHYLUS: I could have wished to meet him otherwhere. We fight not here on equal terms.

DIONYSUS: Why not?

AESCHYLUS: My poetry survived me: his died with him: He's got it here, all handy to recite. Howbeit, if so you wish it, so we'll have it.

DIONYSUS: O bring me fire, and bring me frankincense. I'll pray, or e'er the clash of wits begin, To judge the strife with high poetic skill. Meanwhile (to the CHORUS:) invoke the Muses with a song.

CHORUS: O Muses, the daughters divine of Zeus, the immaculate Nine, Who gaze from your mansions serene on intellects subtle and keen, When down to the tournament lists, in bright-polished wit they descend, With wrestling and turnings and twists in the battle of words to contend, O come and behold what the two antagonist poets can do, Whose mouths are the swiftest to teach grand language and filings of speech: For now of their wits is the sternest encounter commencing in earnest.

DIONYSUS: Ye two, put up your prayers before ye start.

AESCHYLUS: Demeter, mistress, nourisher of my soul, O make me worthy of thy mystic rites!

DIONYSUS: (to EURIPIDES:) Now put on incense, you.

EURIPIDES: Excuse me, no; My vows are paid to other gods than these.

DIONYSUS: What, a new coinage of your own?

EURIPIDES: Precisely.

DIONYSUS: Pray then to them, those private gods of yours.

EURIPIDES: Ether, my pasture, volubly-rolling tongue, Intelligent wit and critic nostrils keen, O well and neatly may I trounce his plays!

CHORUS: We also are yearning from these to be learning Some stately measure, some majestic grand Movement telling of conflicts nigh. Now for battle arrayed they stand, Tongues embittered, and anger high. Each has got a venturesome will, Each an eager and nimble mind; One will wield, with artistic skill, Clearcut phrases, and wit refined; Then the other, with words defiant,

152

Stern and strong, like an angry giant Laying on with uprooted trees, Soon will scatter a world of these Superscholastic subtleties.

DIONYSUS: Now then, commence your arguments,   and mind you both display True wit, not metaphors, nor things which any fool could say.

EURIPIDES: As for myself, good people all, I'll tell you by-and-by My own poetic worth and claims; but first of all I'll try To show how this portentous quack   beguiled the silly fools Whose tastes were nurtured, ere he came, in Phrynichus's schools. He'd bring some single mourner on, seated and veiled, 'twould be Achilles, say, or Niobe -the face you could not see- An empty show of tragic woe, who uttered not one thing.

DIONYSUS: 'Tis true.

EURIPIDES: Then in the chorus came, and rattled off a string four continuous lyric odes: the mourner never stirred.

DIONYSUS: I liked it too. I sometimes think that I those mutes preferred To all your chatterers now-a-days.

EURIPIDES: Because, if you must know, You were an ass.

DIONYSUS: An ass, no doubt; what made him do it though?

EURIPIDES: That was his quackery, don't you see,   to set the audience guessing When Niobe would speak; meanwhile, the drama was progressing.

DIONYSUS: The rascal, how he took me in! 'Twas shameful, was it not? (To AESCHYLUS:) What makes you stamp and fidget so?

EURIPIDES: He's catching it so hot. So when he had humbugged thus awhile, and now his wretched play Was halfway through, a dozen words, great wild-bull words, he'd say, Fierce Bugaboos, with bristling crests,   and shaggy eyebrows too, Which not a soul could understand.

153

AESCHYLUS: O heavens!

DIONYSUS: Be quiet, do.

EURIPIDES: But not one single word was clear.

DIONYSUS: St! don't your teeth be gnashing.

EURIPIDES: 'Twas all Scamanders, moated camps, and griffin-eagles flashing
In burnished copper on the shields,
chivalric-precipice-high Expressions, hard to comprehend.

DIONYSUS: Aye, by the Powers, and Full many a sleepless night have spent
in anxious thought, because I'd find the tawny cock-horse out, what sort of bird
it was!

AESCHYLUS: It was a sign, you stupid dolt, engraved the ships upon.

DIONYSUS: Eryxis I supposed it was, Philoxenus's son.

EURIPIDES: Now really should a cock be brought into a tragic play?

AESCHYLUS: You enemy gods and men, what was your practice, pray?

EURIPIDES: No cock-horse in my plays, by Zeus, no goat-stag there you'll
see, Such figures as are blazoned forth in Median tapestry. When first I took
the art from you, bloated and swoln, poor thing, With turgid gasconading words
and heavy dieting, First I reduced and toned her down, and made her slim and
neat With wordlets and with exercise and poultices of beet, And next a dose of
chatterjuice, distilled from books, I gave her, And monodies she took, with
sharp Cephisophon for flavour. I never used haphazard words, or plunged
abruptly in; Who entered first explained at large the drama's origin And source.

AESCHYLUS: Its source, I really trust, was better than your own.

154

EURIPIDES: Then from the very opening lines no idleness was shown; The mistress talked with all her might, the servant talked as much, The master talked, the maiden talked, the beldame talked. An outrage was not death your due?

EURIPIDES: No, by Apollo, no: That was my democratic way.

DIONYSUS: Ah, let that topic go. Your record is not there, my friend, particularly good.

EURIPIDES: Then next I taught all these to speak.

AESCHYLUS: You did so, and I would That ere such mischief you had wrought, your very rungs had split.

EURIPIDES: Canons of verse I introduced, and neatly chiselled wit; To look, to scan: to plot, to plan: to twist, to turn, to woo: On all to spy; in all to pry.

AESCHYLUS: You did: I say so too.

EURIPIDES: I showed them scenes of common life, the things we know and see, Where any blunder would at once by all detected be. I never blustered on, or took their breath and wits away By Cycnuses or Memnons clad in terrible array, With bells upon their horses' heads, the audience to dismay. Look at his pupils, look at mine: and there the contrast view. Uncouth Megaenetus is his, and rough Phormisius too; Great long-beard-lance-and-trumpet-men, flesh-tearers with the pine: But natty smart Theramenes, and Cleitophon are mine.

DIONYSUS: Theramenes? a clever man and wonderfully sly: Immerse him in a flood of ills, he'll soon be high and dry, "A Kian with a kappa, sir, not Chian with a chi."

EURIPIDES: I taught them all these knowing ways By chopping logic in my plays, And making all my speakers try To reason out the How and Why. So now the people trace the springs, The sources and the roots of things, And

155

manage all their households to Far better than they used to do, Scanning and searching "What's amiss?" And, "Why was that?" And, "How is this?"

DIONYSUS: Ay, truly, never now a man Comes home, but he begins to scan; And to his household loudly cries, "Why, where's my pitcher? What's the matter? 'Tis dead and my last year's platter. Who gnawed these olives? Bless the sprat, Who nibbled off the head of that? And where's the garlic vanished, pray, I purchased only yesterday?" -Whereas, of old, our stupid youths Would sit, with open mouths and eyes, Like any dull-brained Mammacouths.

CHORUS: "All this thou beholdest, Achilles our boldest." And what wilt thou reply? Draw tight the rein Lest that fiery soul of thine Whirl thee out of the listed plain, Past the olives, and o'er the line. Dire and grievous the charge he brings. See thou answer him, noble heart, Not with passionate bickerings. Shape thy course with a sailor's art, Reef the canvas, shorten the sails, Shift them edgewise to shun the gales. When the breezes are soft and low, Then, well under control, you'll go Quick and quicker to strike the foe. O first of all the Hellenic bards high loftily-towering verse to rear, And tragic phrase from the dust to raise, pour forth thy fountain with right good cheer.

AESCHYLUS: My wrath is hot at this vile mischance, and my spirit revolts at the thought that Must bandy words with a fellow like him: but lest he should vaunt that I can't reply- Come, tell me what are the points for which a noble poet our praise obtains.

EURIPIDES: For his ready wit, and his counsels sage, and because the citizen folk he trains To be better townsmen and worthier men.

AESCHYLUS: If then you have done the very reverse, Found noble-hearted and virtuous men, and altered them, each and all, for the worse, Pray what is the meed you deserve to get?

DIONYSUS: Nay, ask not him. He deserves to die.

AESCHYLUS: For just consider what style of men he received from me, great six-foot-high Heroical souls, who never would blench from a townsman's duties in peace or war; Not idle loafers, or low buffoons, or rascally scamps such as now they are. But men who were breathing spears and helms, and the snow-white plume in its crested pride, The greave, and the dart, and the warrior's heart in its sevenfold casing of tough bull-hide.

DIONYSUS: He'll stun me, I know, with his armoury-work; this business is going from bad to worse.

EURIPIDES: And how did you manage to make them so grand, exalted, and brave with your wonderful verse?

DIONYSUS: Come, Aeschylus, answer, and don't stand mute in your self-willed pride and arrogant spleen.

AESCHYLUS: A drama I wrote with the War-god filled.

DIONYSUS: Its name?

AESCHYLUS: 'Tis the Seven against Thebes that I mean. Which whoso beheld, with eagerness swelled to rush to the battlefield there and then.

DIONYSUS: O that was a scandalous thing you did! You have made the Thebans mightier men, More eager by far for the business of war. Now, therefore, receive this punch on the head.

AESCHYLUS: Ah, ye might have practised the same yourselves, but ye turned to other pursuits instead. Then next the Persians I wrote, in praise of the noblest deed that the world can show, And each man longed for the victor's wreath, to fight and to vanquish his country's foe.

DIONYSUS: I was pleased, I own, when I heard their moan for old Darius, their great king, dead; When they smote together their hands, like this, and "Evir alake" the chorus said.

AESCHYLUS: Aye, such are the poet's appropriate works: and just consider how all along From the very first they have wrought you good, the noble bards,

157

the masters of song. First, Orpheus taught you religious rites, and from bloody murder to stay your hands: Musaeus healing and oracle lore; and Hesiod all the culture of lands, The time to gather, the time to plough. And gat not Homer his glory divine By singing of valour, and honour, and right, and the sheen of the battle-extended line, The ranging of troops and the arming of men?

DIONYSUS: O ay, but he didn't teach that, I opine, To Pantacles; when he was leading the show I couldn't imagine what he was at, He had fastened his helm on the top of his head, he was trying to fasten his plume upon that.

AESCHYLUS: But others, many and brave, he taught, of whom was Lamachus, hero true; And thence my spirit the impress took, and many a lion-heart chief I drew, Patrocluses, Teucers, illustrious names; for I fain the citizen-folk would spur To stretch themselves to their measure and height, whenever the trumpet of war they hear. But Phaedras and Stheneboeas? No! no harlotry business deformed my plays. And none can say that ever I drew a love-sick woman in all my days.

EURIPIDES: For you no lot or portion had got in Queen Aphrodite.

AESCHYLUS: Thank Heaven for that. But ever on you and yours, my friend, the mighty goddess mightily sat; Yourself she cast to the ground at last.

DIONYSUS: O ay, that uncommonly pat. You showed how cuckolds are made, and lo, you were struck yourself by the very same fate.

EURIPIDES: But say, you cross-grained censor of mine, how my Stheneboeas could harm the state.

AESCHYLUS: Full many a noble dame, the wife of a noble citizen, hemlock took, And died, unable the shame and sin of your Bellerophon-scenes to brook.

EURIPIDES: Was then, I wonder, the tale I told of Phaedra's passionate love untrue?

AESCHYLUS: Not so: but tales of incestuous vice the sacred poet should hide from view, Nor ever exhibit and blazon forth on the public stage to the public ken. For boys a teacher at school is found, but we, the poets, are teachers of men. We are hound things honest and pure to speak.

EURIPIDES: And to speak great Lycabettuses, pray, And massive blocks of Parnassian rocks, is that things honest and pure to say? In human fashion we ought to speak.

AESCHYLUS: Alas, poor witling, and can't you see That for mighty thoughts and heroic aims, the words themselves must appropriate be? And grander belike on the ear should strike the speech of heroes and godlike powers, Since even the robes that invest their limbs are statelier, grander robes than ours. Such was my plan: but when you began, you spoilt and degraded it all.

AESCHYLUS: Your kings in tatters and rags you dressed, and brought them on, a beggarly show, To move, forsooth, our pity and ruth.

EURIPIDES: And what was the harm, I should like to know.

AESCHYLUS: No more will a wealthy citizen now equip for the state a galley of war. He wraps his limbs in tatters and rags, and whines he is "poor, too poor by far."

DIONYSUS: But under his rags he is wearing a vest, as woolly and soft as a man could wish. Let him gull the state, and he's off to the mart; an eager, extravagant buyer of fish.

AESCHYLUS: Moreover to prate, to harangue, to debate, is now the ambition of all in the state. Each exercise-ground is in consequence found deserted and empty: to evil repute Your lessons have brought our youngsters, and taught our sailors to challenge, discuss, and refute The orders they get from their captains and yet, when I was alive, I protest that the knaves Knew nothing at all, save for rations to call, and to sing "Rhyppapae" as they pulled through the waves.

159

DIONYSUS: And bedad to let fly from their sterns in the eye of the fellow who tugged at the undermost oar, And a jolly young messmate with filth to besmirch, and to land for a filching adventure ashore; But now they harangue, and dispute, and won't row And idly and aimlessly float to and fro.

AESCHYLUS: Of what ills is lie not the creator and cause? Consider the scandalous scenes that he draws, His bawds, and his panders, his women who give Give birth in the sacredest shrine, Whilst others with brothers are wedded and bedded, And others opine That "not to be living" is truly "to live." And therefore our city is swarming to-day With clerks and with demagogue-monkeys, who play Their jackanape tricks at all times, in all places, Deluding the people of Athens; but none Has training enough in athletics to run With the torch in his
hand at the races.

DIONYSUS: By the Powers, you are right! At the Panathenaea I laughed till I felt like a potsherd to see Pale, paunchy young gentleman pounding along, With his head butting forward, the last of the throng, In the direst of straits; and behold at the gates, The Ceramites flapped him, and smacked him, and slapped him, In the ribs, and the loin, and the flank, and the groin, And still, as they spanked him, he puffed and he panted, Till at one mighty cuff, he discharged such a puff That he blew out his torch and levanted.

CHORUS: Dread the battle, and stout the combat, mighty and manifold looms the war. Hard to decide is the fight they're waging, One like a stormy tempest raging, One alert in the rally and skirmish, clever to parry and foin and spar. Nay but don't be content to sit Always in one position only: many the fields for your keen-edged wit. On then, wrangle in every way, Argue, battle, be flayed and flay, Old and new from your stores display, Yea, and strive with venturesome daring something subtle and neat to say. Fear ye this, that to-day's spectators lack the grace of artistic lore, Lack the knowledge they need for taking All the points ye will soon be making? Fear it not: the alarm is groundless: that, be sure, is the case no more. All have fought the campaign ere this: Each a book of the words is holding; never a single point they'll miss. Bright their natures, and now, I ween, Newly whetted, and sharp, and keen.

160

Dread not any defect of wit, Battle away without misgiving, sure that the audience, at least, are fit.

EURIPIDES: Well then I'll turn me to your prologues now, Beginning first to test the first beginning Of this fine poet's plays. Why he's obscure Even in the enunciation of the facts.

DIONYSUS: Which of them will you test?

EURIPIDES: Many: but first Give us that famous one from the Oresteia.

DIONYSUS: St! Silence all! Now, Aeschylus, begin.

AESCHYLUS: "Grave Hermes, witnessing a father's power, Be thou my saviour and mine aid to-day, For here I come and hither I return."

DIONYSUS: Any fault there?

EURIPIDES: A dozen faults and more.

DIONYSUS: Eh! why the lines are only three in all.

EURIPIDES: But everyone contains a score of faults.

DIONYSUS: Now Aeschylus, keep silent; if you don't You won't get off with three iambic lines.

AESCHYLUS: Silent for him!

DIONYSUS: If my advice you'll take.

EURIPIDES: Why, at first starting here's a fault skyhigh.

AESCHYLUS: (to DIONYSUS:) You see your folly?

DIONYSUS: Have your way; I care not.

161

AESCHYLUS: (to EURIPIDES:) What is my fault?

EURIPIDES: Begin the lines again.

AESCHYLUS: "Grave Hermes, witnessing a father's power-"

EURIPIDES: And this beside his murdered father's grave Orestes speaks?

AESCHYLUS: I say not otherwise.

EURIPIDES: Then does he mean that when his father fell By craft and violence at a woman's hand, The god of craft was witnessing the deed?

AESCHYLUS: It was not he: it was the Helper Hermes He called the grave: and this he showed by adding It was his sire's prerogative he held.

EURIPIDES: Why this is worse than all. If from his father He held this office grave, why then-

DIONYSUS: He was A graveyard rifler on his father's side.

AESCHYLUS: Bacchus, the wine you drink is stale and fusty.

DIONYSUS: Give him another: (to EURIPIDES:) you, look out for faults.

AESCHYLUS: "Be thou my saviour and mine aid to-day, For here I come, and hither I return."

EURIPIDES: The same thing twice says clever Aeschylus.

DIONYSUS: How twice?

EURIPIDES: Why, just consider: I'll explain. "I come, says he; and "I return," says he: It's the same thing, to "come" and to "return."

162

DIONYSUS: Aye, just as if you said, "Good fellow, tend me A kneading trough: likewise, a trough to knead in."

AESCHYLUS: It is not so, you everlasting talker, They're not the same, the words are right enough.

DIONYSUS: How so? inform me how you use the words.

AESCHYLUS: A man, not banished from his home, may "come" To any land, with no especial chance. A home-bound exile both "returns" and "comes."

DIONYSUS: O good, by Apollo! What do you say, Euripides, to that?

EURIPIDES: I say Orestes never did "return." He came in secret: nobody recalled him.

DIONYSUS: O good, by Hermes I (Aside) I've not the least suspicion what he means.

EURIPIDES: Repeat another line.

DIONYSUS: Ay, Aeschylus, Repeat one instantly: you, mark what's wrong.

AESCHYLUS: "Now on this funeral mound I call my rather To hear, to hearken.

EURIPIDES: There he is again. To "hear," to "hearken"; the same thing, exactly.

DIONYSUS: Aye, but he's speaking to the dead, you knave, Who cannot hear us though we call them thrice.

AESCHYLUS: And how do you make your prologues?

EURIPIDES: You shall hear; And if you find one single thing said twice, Or any useless padding, spit upon me.

163

DIONYSUS: Well, fire away: I'm all agog to hear Your very accurate and faultless prologues.

EURIPIDES: "A happy man was Oedipus at first-

AESCHYLUS: Not so, by Zeus; a most unhappy man. Who, not yet born nor yet conceived, Apollo Foretold would be his father's murderer. How could he be a happy man at first?

EURIPIDES: "Then he became the wretchedest of men."

AESCHYLUS: Not so, by Zeus; he never ceased to be. No sooner born, than they exposed the babe, (And that in winter), in an earthen crock, Lest he should grow a man, and slay his father. Then with both ankles pierced and swoln, he limped Away to Polybus: still young, he married An ancient crone, and her his mother too. Then scratched out both his eyes.

DIONYSUS: Happy indeed Had he been Erasinides's colleague!

EURIPIDES: Nonsense; I say my prologues are firstrate.

AESCHYLUS: Nay then, by Zeus, no longer line by line I'll maul your phrases: but with heaven to aid I'll smash your prologues with a bottle of oil.

EURIPIDES: You mine with a bottle of oil?

AESCHYLUS: With only one. You frame your prologues so that each and all Fit in with a "bottle of oil," or "coverlet-skin," Or "reticule-bag." I'll prove it here, and now.

EURIPIDES: You'll prove it? You?

AESCHYLUS: I will.

DIONYSUS: Well then, begin.

164

EURIPIDES: "Aegyptus, sailing with his fifty sons, As ancient legends mostly tell the tale, Touching at Argos"

AESCHYLUS: Lost his bottle of oil.

EURIPIDES: Hang it, what's that? Confound that bottle of oil! Give him another: let him try again.

EURIPIDES: "Bacchus, who, clad in fawnskins, leaps and bounds torch and thyrsus in the choral dance along Parnassus"

AESCHYLUS: Lost his bottle of oil.

DIONYSUS: Ah me, we are stricken-with that bottle again! Pooh, pooh, that's nothing. I've a prologue He'll never tack his bottle of oil to this: "No man is blest in every single thing. One is of noble birth, but lacking means. Another, baseborn,"

AESCHYLUS: Lost his bottle of oil.

DIONYSUS: Euripides!

EURIPIDES: Well?

DIONYSUS: Lower your sails, my boy; This bottle of is going to blow a gale.

EURIPIDES: O, by Demeter, I care one bit; Now from his hands I'll strike that bottle of oil.

DIONYSUS: Go on then, go: but ware the bottle of oil.

EURIPIDES: "Once Cadmus, quitting the Sidonian town, Agenor's offspring"

AESCHYLUS: Lost his bottle of oil.

DIONYSUS: O pray, my man, buy off that bottle of oil, Or else he'll smash our prologues all to bits.

EURIPIDES: I buy of him?

DIONYSUS: If my advice you'll take.

EURIPIDES: No, no, I've many a prologue yet to say, To which he can't tack on his bottle of oil. "Pelops, the son of Tantalus, while driving His mares to Pisa"

AESCHYLUS: Lost his bottle of oil.

DIONYSUS: There! he tacked on the bottle of oil again. O for heaven's sake, pay him its price, dear boy; You'll get it for an obol, spick and span.

EURIPIDES: Not yet, by Zeus; I've plenty of prologues left. "Oeneus once reaping"

AESCHYLUS: Lost his bottle of oil.

EURIPIDES: Pray let me finish one entire line first. "Oeneus once reaping an abundant harvest, Offering the firstfruits"

AESCHYLUS: Lost his bottle of oil.

DIONYSUS: What, in the act of offering? Fie! Who stole it?

EURIPIDES: O don't keep bothering! Let him try with "Zeus, as by Truth's own voice the tale is told,"

DIONYSUS: No, he'll cut in with "Lost his bottle of oil" bottle Those bottles of oil on all your prologues seem To gather and grow, like styes upon the eye. Turn to his melodies now for goodness' sake.

166

EURIPIDES: O I can easily show that he's a poor Melody-maker; makes all alike.

CHORUS: What, O what will be done! Strange to think that he dare Blame the bard who has won, More than all in our days, Fame and praise for his lays, Lays so many and fair. Much I marvel to hear What the charge he will bring 'Gainst our tragedy king; Yea for himself do fear.

EURIPIDES: Wonderful lays! O yes, you'll see directly. I'll cut down all his metrical strains to one.

DIONYSUS: And I, I'll take some pebbles, and keep count.

A slight pause, during which the music of a flute is heard. The music continues to the end of line [EURIPIDES: -Hush! the bee...] as an accompaniment to the recitative.

EURIPIDES: "Lord of Phthia, Achilles, why hearing the voice of the hero-dividing Hah! smiting! approachest thou not to the rescue? We, by the lake who abide, are adoring our ancestor Hermes. Hah! smiting! approachest thou not to the rescue?"

DIONYSUS: O Aeschylus, twice art thou smitten I

EURIPIDES: "Hearken to me, great king; yea, hearken Atreides, thou noblest of the Achaeans. Hah! smiting! approachest thou not to the rescue?

DIONYSUS: Thrice, Aeschylus, thrice art thou smitten!

EURIPIDES: "Hush! the bee-wardens are here: they will quickly the Temple of Artemis open. Hah! smiting! approachest thou not to the rescue? I will expound (for I know it) the omen the chieftains encountered. Hah! smiting! approachest thou not to the rescue?"

DIONYSUS: O Zeus and King, the terrible lot of smittings! I'll to the bath: I'm very sure my kidneys Are quite inflamed and swoln with all these smitings.

167

EURIPIDES: Wait till you've heard another batch of lays Culled from his lyre-accompanied melodies.

DIONYSUS: Go on then, go: but no more smitings, please.

EURIPIDES: "How the twin-throned powers of Achaea, the lords of the mighty Hellenes. O phlattothrattophlattothrat! Sendeth the Sphinx, the unchancy, the chieftainness bloodhound. O phlattothrattophlattothratt launcheth fierce with brand and hand the avengers the terrible eagle. O phlattothrattophlattothrat! So for the swift-winged hounds of the air he provided a booty. O phlattothrattophlattothrat! The throng down-bearing on Aias. O phlattothrattophlattotbrat!"

DIONYSUS: Whence comes that phlattothrat? From Marathon, or Where picked you up these cable-twister's strains?

AESCHYLUS: From noblest source for noblest ends brought them, Unwilling in the Muses' holy field The self-same flowers as Phrynichus to cull. But he from all things rotten draws his lays, From Carian flutings, catches of Meletus, Dance-music, dirges. You shall hear directly. Bring me the lyre. Yet wherefore need a lyre For songs like these? Where's she that bangs and jangles Her castanets?

EURIPIDES: Muse, Present yourself: fit goddess for fit verse.

DIONYSUS: The Muse herself can't be a wanton? No!

AESCHYLUS: Halycons, who by the ever-rippling Waves of the sea are babbling, Dewing your plumes with the drops that fall From wings in the salt spray dabbling. Spiders, ever with twir-r-r-r-rling fingers Weaving the warp and the woof, Little, brittle, network, fretwork, Under the coigns of the roof. The minstrel shuttle's care. Where in the front of the dark-prowed ships Yarely the flute-loving dolphin skips. Races here and oracles there. And the joy of the young vines smiling, And the tendril of grapes, care-beguiling. O embrace me, my child, O embrace me. (To DIONYSUS:) You see this foot?

DIONYSUS: I do.

AESCHYLUS: And this?

DIONYSUS: And that one too.

AESCHYLUS: (to EURIPIDES:) You, such stuff who compile, Dare my songs to upbraid; You, whose songs in the style Of Cyrene's embraces are made.

The FROGS: So much for them: but still I'd like to show The way in which your monodies are framed "O darkly-light mysterious Night, What may this Vision mean, Sent from the world unseen With baleful omens rife; A thing of lifeless life, A child of sable night, A ghastly curdlinisight, In black funereal veils, With murder, murder in its eyes, And great enormous nails? Light ye the lanterns, my MAID: ens, and dipping your jugs in the stream, Draw me the dew of the water, and heat it to boiling and steam; So will I wash me away the ill effects of my dream. God of the sea! My dream's come true. Ho, lodgers, ho, This portent view. Glyce has vanished, carrying off my cock, My cock that crew! O Mania, help! O Oreads of the rock Pursue! pursue! For I, poor girl, was working within, Holding my distaff heavy and full, Twir-r-r-r-rling my hand as the threads I spin, Weaving an excellent bobbin of wool; Thinking 'To-morrow I'll go to the fair, In the dusk of the morn, and be selling it there.' But he to the blue up flew, up flew, on the lightliest tips of his wings outspread; To me he bequeathed but woe, but woe, And tears, sad tears, from my eyes o'erflow, Which I, the bereaved, must shed, must shed. O children of Ida, sons of Crete, Grasping your bows to the rescue come; Twinkle about on your restless feet, Stand in a circle around her home. O Artemis, thou maid divine, Dictynna, huntress, fair to see, O bring that keen-nosed pack of thine, And hunt through all the house with me. O Hecate, with flameful brands, O Zeus's daughter, arm thine hands, Those swiftliest hands, both right and left; Thy rays on Glyce's cottage throw That I serenely there may go, And search by moonlight for the theft."

DIONYSUS: Enough of both your odes.

169

AESCHYLUS: Enough for me. Now would I bring the fellow to the scales. That, that alone, shall test our poetry now, And prove whose words are weightiest, his or mine.

DIONYSUS: Then both come hither, since I needs must weigh The art poetic like a pound of cheese. Here a large balance is brought out and placed upon the stage.

CHORUS: O the labour these wits go through I O the wild, extravagant, new, Wonderful things they are going to do! Who but they would ever have thought of it? Why, if a man had happened to meet me Out in the street, and intelligence brought of it, I should have thought he was trying to cheat me; Thought that his story was false and deceiving. That were a tale I could never believe in.

DIONYSUS: Each of you stand beside his scale.

AESCHYLUS and **EURIPIDES**: We're here.

DIONYSUS: And grasp it firmly whilst ye speak your lines, Each holds his own scale steady while he speaks his line into it. And don't let go until I cry "Cuckoo."

AESCHYLUS and **EURIPIDES**: Ready!

DIONYSUS: Now speak your lines into the scale.

EURIPIDES: "O that the Argo had not winged her way-"

AESCHYLUS: "River Spercheius, cattle-grazing haunts-"

DIONYSUS: Cuckoo! let go. O look, by far the lowest His scale sinks down.

EURIPIDES: Why, how came that about?

DIONYSUS: He threw a river in, like some wool-seller Wetting his wool, to make it weigh the more. But threw in a light and winged word.

EURIPIDES: Come, let him match another verse with mine.

DIONYSUS: Each to his scale.

AESCHYLUS and **EURIPIDES**: We're ready.

DIONYSUS: Speak your lines.

EURIPIDES: "Persuasion's only shrine is eloquent speech."

AESCHYLUS: "Death loves not gifts, alone amongst the gods."

DIONYSUS: Let go, let go. Down goes his scale again. He threw in Death, the heaviest ill of all.

EURIPIDES: And I Persuasion, the most lovely word.

DIONYSUS: A vain and empty sound, devoid of sense. Think of some heavier-weighted line of yours, To drag your scale down: something strong and big.

EURIPIDES: Where have I got one? Where? Let's see.

DIONYSUS: I'll tell you. "Achilles threw two singles and a four." Come, speak your lines: this is your last set-to.

EURIPIDES: "In his right hand he grasped an iron-clamped mace."

AESCHYLUS: "Chariot on chariot, corpse on corpse was hurled."

DIONYSUS: There now! again he has done you.

EURIPIDES: Done me? How?

DIONYSUS: He threw two chariots and two corpses in; Five-score Egyptians could not lift that weight.

AESCHYLUS: No more of "line for line"; let him-himself, His children, wife, Cephisophon-get in, With all his books collected in his arms, Two lines of mine shall overweigh the lot.

DIONYSUS: Both are my friends; I can't decide between them: I don't desire to be at odds with either: One is so clever,
one delights me so.

PLUTO: (coming forward) Then you'll effect nothing for which you came?

DIONYSUS: And how, if I decide?

PLUTO: Then take the winner; So will your journey not be made in vain.

DIONYSUS: Heaven bless your Highness! Listen, I came down After a poet.

EURIPIDES: To what end? The city, saved, may keep her choral games. Now then, whichever of you two shall best Advise the city, he shall come with me. And first of Alcibiades, let each Say what he thinks; the city travails sore.

DIONYSUS: What does she think herself about him? She loves, and hates, and longs to have him back. But give me your advice about the man.

EURIPIDES: I loathe a townsman who is slow to aid, And swift to hurt, his town: who ways and means Finds for himself, but finds not for the state.

DIONYSUS: Poseidon, but that's smart! (to AESCHYLUS:) And what say you?

AESCHYLUS: 'Twere best to rear no lion in the state: But having reared, 'tis best to humour him.

DIONYSUS: By Zeus the Saviour, still I can't decide. One is so clever, and so clear the other. But once again. Let each in turn declare What plan of safety for the state ye've got.

EURIPIDES: First with Cinesias wing Cleocritus, Then zephyrs waft them o'er the watery plain.

DIONYSUS: A funny sight, I own: but where's the sense?

EURIPIDES: If, when the fleets engage, they holding cruets Should rain down vinegar in the foemen's eyes,] I know, and I can tell you.

DIONYSUS: Tell away.

EURIPIDES: When things, mistrusted now, shall trusted be, And trusted things, mistrusted.

DIONYSUS: How! I don't Quite comprehend. Be clear, and not so clever.

EURIPIDES: If we mistrust those citizens of ours Whom now we trust, and those employ whom now We don't employ, the city will be saved. If on our present tack we fail, we surely Shall find salvation in the opposite course.

DIONYSUS: Good, O Palamedes! Good, you genius you. Is this your cleverness or Cephisophon's?

EURIPIDES: This is my own: the cruet-plan was his.

DIONYSUS: (to AESCHYLUS:) Now, you.

AESCHYLUS: But tell me whom the city uses. The good and useful?

DIONYSUS: What are you dreaming of? She hates and loathes them.

AESCHYLUS: Does she love the bad?

173

DIONYSUS: Not love them, no: she uses them perforce.

AESCHYLUS: How can one save a city such as this, Whom neither frieze nor woollen tunic suits?

DIONYSUS: O, if to earth you rise, find out some way.

AESCHYLUS: There will I speak: I cannot answer here.

DIONYSUS: Nay, nay; send up your guerdon from below.

AESCHYLUS: When they shall count the enemy's soil their And theirs the enemy's: when they know that ships Are their true wealth, their so-called wealth delusion.

DIONYSUS: Aye, but the justices suck that down, you know.

PLUTO: Now then, decide.

DIONYSUS: I will; and thus I'll do it. I'll choose the man in whom my soul delights.

EURIPIDES: O, recollect the gods by whom you swore You'd take me home again; and choose your friends.

DIONYSUS: 'Twas my tongue swore; my choice is- Aeschylus.

EURIPIDES: Hah! what have you done?

DIONYSUS: Done? Given the victor's prize To Aeschylus; why not?

EURIPIDES: And do you dare Look in my face, after that shameful deed?

DIONYSUS: What's shameful, if the audience think not so? Have you no heart? Wretch, would you leave me dead?

DIONYSUS: Who knows if death be life, and life be death, And breath be mutton broth, and sleep a sheepskin?

PLUTO: Now, Dionysus, come ye in,

DIONYSUS: What for?

PLUTO: And sup before ye go.

DIONYSUS: A bright idea. I'faith, I'm nowise indisposed for that.   Exit Aeschylus, Euripides, Pluto, and Dionysus.

CHORUS: Blest the man who possesses Keen intelligent mind. This full often we find. He, the bard of renown, Now to earth reascends, Goes, a joy to his town, Goes, a joy to his friends, Just because he possesses Keen intelligent mind. Right it is and befitting, Not, by Socrates sitting, Idle talk to pursue, Stripping tragedy-art of All things noble and true. Surely the mind to school Fine-drawn quibbles to seek, Fine-set phrases to speak, Is but the part of a fool Re-enter Pluto and Aeschylus.

PLUTO: Farewell then Aeschylus, great and wise, Go, save our state by the maxims rare Of thy noble thought; and the fools chastise, For many a fool dwells there. And this (handing him a rope) to Cleophon give, my friend, And this to the revenue-raising crew, Nichomachus, Myrmex, next I send, And this to Archenomus too. And bid them all that without delay, To my realm of the dead they hasten away. For if they loiter above, I swear I'll come myself and arrest them there. And branded and fettered the slaves shall With the vilest rascal in all the town, Adeimantus, son of Leucolophus, down, Down, down to the darkness below.

AESCHYLUS: I take the mission. This chair of mine Meanwhile to Sophocles here commit, (For I count him next in our craft divine,) Till I come once more by thy side to sit. But as for that rascally scoundrel there, That low buffoon, that worker of ill, O let him not sit in my vacant chair, Not even against his will.

175

PLUTO: (to the CHORUS) Escort him up with your mystic throngs, While the holy torches quiver and blaze. Escort him up with his own sweet gongs, And his noble festival lays.

CHORUS: First, as the poet triumphant is passing away to the light, Grant him success on his journey, ye powers that are ruling below. Grant that he find for the city good counsels to guide her aright; So we at last shall be freed from the anguish, the fear, and the woe, Freed from the onsets of war. Let Cleophon now and his band Battle, if battle they must, far away in their own fatherland.

THE END

THE BIRDS

CHARACTERS

EUELPIDES
PITHETAERUS
TROCHILUS , Servant to Epops
Epops (the Hoopoe)
A BIRD:
A HERALD
A PRIEST
A POET
AN ORACLE-MONGER
METON , a Geometrician
AN INSPECTOR
A DEALER IN DECREES
IRIS
A PARRICIDE
CINESIAS: , a Dithyrambic POET
AN INFORMER
PROMETHEUS
POSIDON
TRIBALLUS
HERACLES
SLAVES OF PITHETAERUS
MESSENGERS
CHORUS OF BIRDS

THE BIRDS

BIRDS: (SCENE:-A wild and desolate region; only thickets, rocks, and a single tree are seen. EUELPIDES and PITHETAERUS enter, each with a bird in his hand.)

EUELPIDES: (to his jay) Do you think I should walk straight for yon tree?

PITHETAERUS: (to his crow) Cursed beast, what are you croaking to me?...to retrace my steps?

EUELPIDES: Why, you wretch, we are wandering at random, we are exerting ourselves only to return to the same spot; we're wasting our time.

PITHETAERUS: To think that I should trust to this crow, which has made me cover more than a thousand furlongs!

EUELPIDES: And that I, in obedience to this jay, should have worn my toes down to the nails!

PITHETAERUS: If only I knew where we were....

EUELPIDES: Could you find your country again from here?

PITHETAERUS: No, I feel quite sure I could not, any more than could Execestides find his.

EUELPIDES: Alas!

PITHETAERUS: Aye, aye, my friend, it's surely the road of "alases" we are following.

EUELPIDES: That Philocrates, the bird-seller, played us a scurvy trick, when he pretended these two guides could help us to find Tereus, the Epops, who is a bird, without being born of one. He has indeed sold us this jay, a true son of Tharrhelides, for an obolus, and this crow for three, but what can they do? Why,

178

nothing whatever but bite and scratch! (To his jay) What's the matter with you then, that you keep opening your beak? Do you want us to fling ourselves headlong down these rocks? There is no road that way.

PITHETAERUS: Not even the vestige of a trail in any direction

EUELPIDES: And what does the crow say about the road to follow?

PITHETAERUS: By Zeus, it no longer croaks the same thing it did.

EUELPIDES: And which way does it tell us to go now?

PITHETAERUS: It says that, by dint of gnawing, it will devour my fingers.

EUELPIDES: What misfortune is ours! we strain every nerve to get to the crows, do everything we can to that end, and we cannot find our way! Yes, spectators, our madness is quite different from that of Sacas. He is not a citizen, and would fain be one at any cost; we, on the contrary, born of an honourable tribe and family and living in the midst of our fellow-citizens, we have fled from our country as hard as ever we could go. It's not that we hate it; we recognize it to be great and rich, likewise that everyone has the right to ruin himself paying taxes; but the crickets only chirrup among the fig-trees for a month or two, whereas the Athenians spend their whole lives in chanting forth judgments from their law-courts. That is why we started off with a basket, a stew-pot and some myrtle boughs! and have come to seek a quiet country in which to settle. We are going to Tereus, the Epops, to learn from him, whether, in his aerial flights, he has noticed some town of this kind.

PITHETAERUS: Here! look!

EUELPIDES: What's the matter?

PITHETAERUS: Why, the crow has been directing me to something up there for some time now.

179

EUELPIDES: And the jay is also opening it beak and craning its neck to show me I know not what. Clearly, there are some birds about here. We shall soon know, if we kick up a noise to start them.

PITHETAERUS: Do you know what to do? Knock your leg against this rock.

EUELPIDES: And you your head to double the noise.

PITHETAERUS: Well then use a stone instead; take one and hammer with it.

EUELPIDES: Good idea! (He does so.) Ho there, within!
Slave! slave!

PITHETAERUS: What's that, friend! You say, "slave," to summon Epops? It would be much better to shout, "Epops, Epops!

EUELPIDES: Well then, Epops! Must I knock again? Epops!

TROCHILUS: (rushing out of a thicket) Who's there? Who calls my master?

PITHETAERUS: (in terror) Apollo the Deliverer! what an enormous beak! (He defecates. In the confusion both the jay and the crow fly away.)

TROCHILUS: (equally frightened) Good god! they are bird-catchers.

EUELPIDES: (reassuring himself) But is it so terrible? Wouldn't it be better to explain things?

TROCHILUS: (also reassuring himself) You're done for.

EUELPIDES: But we are not men.

TROCHILUS: What are you, then?

EUELPIDES: (defecating also) I am the Fearling, an African bird.

TROCHILUS: You talk nonsense.

EUELPIDES: Well, then, just ask it of my feet.

TROCHILUS: And this other one, what bird is it?
(To PITHETAERUS:) Speak up.

PITHETAERUS: (weakly) I? I am a Crapple, from the land of the pheasants.

EUELPIDES: But you yourself, in the name of the gods! what animal are you?

TROCHILUS: Why, I am a slave-bird.

EUELPIDES: Why, have you been conquered by a cock?

TROCHILUS: No, but when my master was turned into a hoopoe, he begged me to become a bird also, to follow and to serve him.

EUELPIDES: Does a bird need a servant, then?

TROCHILUS: That's no doubt because he was once a man. At times he wants to eat a dish of sardines from Phalerum; I seize my dish and fly to fetch him some. Again he wants some pea-soup; I seize a ladle and a pot and run to get it.

EUELPIDES: This is, then, truly a running-bird. Come, Trochilus, do us the kindness to call your master.

TROCHILUS: Why, he has just fallen asleep after a feed of myrtle-berries and a few grubs.

EUELPIDES: Never mind; wake him up.

TROCHILUS: I an; certain he will be angry. However, I will wake him to please you. (He goes back into the thicket.)

PITHETAERUS: (as soon as TROCHILUS: is out of sight) You cursed brute! why, I am almost dead with terror!

EUELPIDES: Oh! my god! it was sheer fear that made me lose my jay.

PITHETAERUS: Ah! you big coward! were you so frightened that you let go your jay?

EUELPIDES: And did you not lose your crow, when you fell sprawling on the ground? Tell me that.

PITHETAERUS: Not at all.

EUELPIDES: Where is it, then?

PITHETAERUS: It flew away.

EUELPIDES: And you did not let it go? Oh! you brave fellow!

EPOPS: (from within) Open the thicket, that I may go out! (He comes out of the thicket.)

EUELPIDES: By Heracles! what a creature! what plumage! What means this triple crest?

EPOPS: Who wants me?

EUELPIDES: (banteringly) The twelve great gods have used you ill, it seems.

EPOPS: Are you twitting me about my feathers? I have been a man, strangers.

EUELPIDES: It's not you we are jeering at.

EPOPS: At what, then?

EUELPIDES: Why, it's your beak that looks so ridiculous to us.

EPOPS: This is how Sophocles outrages me in his tragedies. Know, I once was Tereus.

EUELPIDES: You were Tereus, and what are you now? A

BIRD: or a peacock?

EPOPS: I am a bird.

EUELPIDES: Then where are your feathers? I don't see any.

EPOPS: They have fallen off.

EUELPIDES: Through illness?

EPOPS: No. All birds moult their feathers, you know, every winter, and others grow in their place. But tell me, who are you?

EUELPIDES: We? We are mortals.

EPOPS: From what country?

EUELPIDES: From the land of the beautful galleys.

EPOPS: Are you dicasts?

EUELPIDES: No, if anything, we are anti-dicasts.

EPOPS: Is that kind of seed sown among you?

EUELPIDES: You have to look hard to find even a little in our fields.

EPOPS: What brings you here?

EUELPIDES: We wish to pay you a visit.

EPOPS: What for?

EUELPIDES: Because you formerly were a man, like we are, formerly you had debts, as we have, formerly you did not want to pay them, like ourselves; furthermore, being turned into a bird, you have when flying seen all lands and seas. Thus you have all human knowledge as well as that of birds. And hence we have come to you to beg you to direct us to some cosy town, in which one can repose as if on thick coverlets.

EPOPS: And are you looking for a greater city than Athens?

EUELPIDES: No, not a greater, but one more pleasant to live in.

EPOPS: Then you are looking for an aristocratic country.

EUELPIDES: I? Not at all! I hold the son of Scellias in horror.

EPOPS: But, after all, what sort of city would please you best?

EUELPIDES: A place where the following would be the most important business: transacted.-Some friend would come knocking at the door quite early in the morning saying, "By Olympian Zeus, be at my house early. as soon as you have bathed, and bring your children too. I am giving a feast, so don't fail, or else don't cross my threshold when I am in distress."

EPOPS: Ah! that's what may be called being fond of hardships! (To PITHETAERUS) And what say you?

PITHETAERUS: My tastes are similar.

EPOPS: And they are?

PITHETAERUS: I want a town where the father of a handsome lad will stop in the street and say to me reproachfully as if I had failed him, "Ah! Is this well done, Stilbonides? You met my son coming from the bath after the gymnasium and you neither spoke to him, nor kissed him, nor took him with you, nor ever once felt his balls. Would anyone call you an old friend of mine?"

EPOPS: Ah! wag, I see you are fond of suffering. But there is a city of delights such as you want. It's on the Red Sea.

EUELPIDES: Oh, no. Not a sea-port, where some fine morning the Salaminian galley can appear, bringing a process-server along. Have you no Greek town you can propose to us?

EPOPS: Why not choose Lepreum in Elis for your settlement?

EUELPIDES: By Zeus! I could not look at Lepreum without disgust, because of Melanthius.

EPOPS: Then, again, there is the Opuntian Locris, where you could live.

EUELPIDES: I would not be Opuntian for a talent. But come, what is it like to live with the birds? You should know pretty well.

EPOPS: Why, it's not a disagreeable life. In the first place, one has no purse.

EUELPIDES: That does away with a lot of roguery.

EPOPS: For food the gardens yield us white sesame, myrtle-berries, poppies and mint.

EUELPIDES: Why, 'tis the life of the newly-wed indeed.

PITHETAERUS: Ha! I am beginning to see a great plan, which will transfer the supreme power to the birds, if you will but take my advice.

EPOPS: Take your advice? In what way?

PITHETAERUS: In what way? Well, firstly, do not fly in all

185

directions with open beak; it is not dignified. Among us, when we see a thoughtless man, we ask, "What sort of bird is this?" and Teleas answers, "It's a man who has no brain, a bird that has lost his head, a creature you cannot catch, for it never remains in any one place."

EPOPS: By Zeus himself! your jest hits the mark. What then is to be done?

PITHETAERUS: Found a city.

EPOPS: We birds? But what sort of city should we build?

PITHETAERUS: Oh, really, really! you talk like such a fool! Look down.

EPOPS: I am looking.

PITHETAERUS: Now look up.

EPOPS: I am looking.

PITHETAERUS: Turn your head round.

EPOPS: Ah! it will be pleasant for me if I end in twisting my neck off!

PITHETAERUS: What have you seen?

EPOPS: The clouds and the sky.

PITHETAERUS: Very well! is not this the pole of the birds then?

EPOPS: How their pole?

PITHETAERUS: Or, if you like it, their place. And since it turns and passes through the whole universe, it is called 'pole.' If you build and fortify it, you will turn your pole into a city. In this way you will reign over mankind as you do over the grasshoppers and you will cause the gods to die of rabid hunger

EPOPS: How so?

PITHETAERUS: The air is between earth and heaven. When we want to go to Delphi, we ask the Boeotians for leave of passage; in the same way, when men sacrifice to the gods, unless the latter pay you tribute, you exercise the right of every nation towards strangers and don't allow the smoke of the sacrifices to pass through your city and territory.

EPOPS: By earth! by snares! by network! by cages! I never heard of anything more cleverly conceived; and, if the other birds approve, I am going to build the city along with you.

PITHETAERUS: Who will explain the matter to them?

EPOPS: You must yourself. Before I came they were quite ignorant, but since have lived with them I have taught them to speak.

PITHETAERUS: But how can they be gathered together?

EPOPS: Easily. I will hasten down to the thicket to waken my dear Procne and as soon as they hear our voices, they will come to us hot wing.

PITHETAERUS: My dear bird, lose no time, please! Fly at once into the thicket and awaken Procne.

(EPOPS rushes into the thicket.)

EPOPS: (from within; singing) Chase off drowsy sleep, dear companion. Let the sacred hymn gush from thy divine throat in melodious strains; roll forth in soft cadence your refreshing melodies to bewail the fate of Itys, which has been the cause of so many tears to us both. Your pure notes rise through the thick leaves of the yew-tree right up to the throne of Zeus, where Phoebus listens to you, Phoebus with his golden hair. And his ivory lyre responds to your plaintive accents; he gathers the choir of the gods and from their immortal lips pours forth a sacred chant of blessed voices. (The flute is played behind the scene, imitating the song of the nightingale.)

187

PITHETAERUS: Oh! by Zeus! what a throat that little bird possesses. He has filled the whole thicket with honey-sweet melody!

EUELPIDES: Hush!

PITHETAERUS: What's the matter?

EUELPIDES: Be still!

PITHETAERUS: What for?

EUELPIDES: Epops is going to sing again.

EPOPS: (in the thicket, singing) Epopopoi popoi popopopoi popoi, here, here, quick, quick, quick, my comrades in the air; all you who pillage the fertile lands of the husbandmen, the numberless tribes who gather and devour the barley seeds, the swift flying race that sings so sweetly. And you whose gentle twitter resounds through the fields with the little cry of tiotictiotiotiotiotiotio; and you who hop about the branches of the ivy in the gardens; the mountain birds, who feed on the wild olive-berries or the arbutus, hurry to come at my call, trioto, trioto, totobrix; you also, who snap up the sharp-stinging gnats in the marshy vales, and you who dwell in the fine plain of Marathon, all damp with dew, and you, the francolin with speckled wings; you too, the halcyons, who flit over the swelling waves of the sea, come hither to hear the tidings; let all the tribes of long-necked birds assemble here; know that a clever old man has come to us, bringing an entirely new idea and proposing great reforms. Let all come to the debate here, here, here, here. Torotorotorotorotix, kikkabau, kikkabau, torotorotorolililix.

PITHETAERUS: Can you see any bird?

EUELPIDES: By Phoebus, no! and yet I am straining my eyesight to scan the sky.

PITHETAERUS: It was hardly worth Epops' while to go and bury himself in the thicket like a hatching plover.

A BIRD: (entering) Torotix, torotix.

PITHETAERUS: Wait, friend, there's a bird.

EUELPIDES: By Zeus, it is a bird, but what kind? Isn't it a peacock?

PITHETAERUS: (as EPOPS comes out of the thicket) Epops will tell us. What is this bird?

EPOPS: It's not one of those you are used to seeing; it's a bird from the marshes.

EUELPIDES: Oh! oh! but he is very handsome with his wings as crimson as flame.

EPOPS: Undoubtedly; indeed he is called flamingo.

EUELPIDES: (excitedly) Hi! I say! You!

PITHETAERUS: What are you shouting for?

EUELPIDES: Why, here's another bird.

PITHETAERUS: Aye, indeed; this one's a foreign bird too. (To EPOPS) What is this bird from beyond the mountains with a look as solemn as it is stupid?

EPOPS: He is called the Mede.

EUELPIDES: The Mede! But, by Heracles, how, if a Mede, has he flown here without a camel?

PITHETAERUS: Here's another bird with a crest. (From here on, the numerous birds that make up the chorus keep rushing in.)

EUELPIDES: Ah! that's curious. I say, Epops, you are not the only one of your kind then?

EPOPS: This bird is the son of Philocles, who is the son of Epops; so that, you see, I am his grandfather; just as one might say, Hipponicus, the son of Callias, who is the son of Hipponicus.

EUELPIDES: Then this bird is Callias! Why, what a lot of his feathers he has lost!

EPOPS: That's because he is honest; so the INFORMER: s set upon him and the women too pluck out his feathers.

EUELPIDES: By Posidon, do you see that many-coloured bird? What is his name?

EPOPS: This one? That's the glutton.

EUELPIDES: Is there another glutton besides Cleonymus? But why, if he is Cleonymus, has he not thrown away his crest? But what is the meaning of all these crests? Have these birds come to contend for the double stadium prize?

EPOPS: They are like the Carians, who cling to the crests of their mountains for greater safety.

PITHETAERUS: Oh, Posidon! look what awful swarms of birds are gathering here!

EUELPIDES: By Phoebus! what a cloud! The entrance to the stage is no longer visible, so closely do they fly together.

PITHETAERUS: Here is the partridge.

EUELPIDES: Why, there is the francolin.

PITHETAERUS: There is the poachard.

EUELPIDES: Here is the kingfisher. (To EPOPS) What's that bird behind the king fisher?

EPOPS: That's the barber.

EUELPIDES: What? A bird a barber?

PITHETAERUS: Why, Sporgilus is one.

EPOPS: Here comes the owl.

EUELPIDES: And who is it brings an owl to Athens?

EPOPS: (pointing to the various species) Here is the magpie, the turtle-dove, the swallow, the horned-owl, the buzzard, the pigeon, the falcon, the ring-dove, the cuckoo, the red-foot, the red-cap, the purple-cap. the kestrel, the diver, the ousel, the osprey, the woodpecker...

PITHETAERUS: Oh! what a lot of birds!

EUELPIDES: Oh! what a lot of blackbirds!

PITHETAERUS: How they scold, how they come rushing up! What a noise! what a noise!

EUELPIDES: Can they be bearing us ill-will?

PITHETAERUS: Oh! there! there! they are opening their beaks and staring at us.

EUELPIDES: Why, so they are.

LEADER OF THE CHORUS: Popopopopopo. Where is he who called me? Where am I to find him?

EPOPS: I have been waiting for you a long while! I never fail in my word to my friends.

LEADER OF THE CHORUS: Titititititititi. What good news have you for me?

EPOPS: Something that concerns our common safety, and that is just as pleasant as it is to the point. Two men, who are subtle reasoners, have come here to seek me.

LEADER OF THE CHORUS: Where? How? What are you saying?

EPOPS: I say, two old men have come from the abode of humans to propose a vast and splendid scheme to us.

LEADER OF THE CHORUS: Oh! it's a horrible, unheard-of crime! What are you saying?

EPOPS: Never let my words scare you.

LEADER OF THE CHORUS: What have you done to me?

EPOPS: I have welcomed two men, who wish to live with us.

LEADER OF THE CHORUS: And you have dared to do that!

EPOPS: Yes, and I am delighted at having done so.

LEADER OF THE CHORUS: And are they already with us?

EPOPS: Just as much as I am.

CHORUS: (singing) Ah! ah! we are betrayed; 'tis sacrilege! Our friend, he who picked up corn-seeds in the same plains as ourselves, has violated our ancient laws; he has broken the oaths that bind all birds; he has laid a snare for me, he has handed us over to the attacks of that impious race which, throughout all time, has never ceased to war against us.

LEADER OF THE CHORUS: As for this traitorous bird, we will decide his case later, but the two old men shall be punished forthwith; we are going to tear them to pieces.

PITHETAERUS: It's all over with us.

EUELPIDES: You are the sole cause of all our trouble. Why did you bring me from down yonder?

PITHETAERUS: To have you with me.

EUELPIDES: Say rather to have me melt into tears.

PITHETAERUS: Go on! you are talking nonsense. How will you weep with your eyes pecked out?

CHORUS: (singing) Io! io! forward to the attack, throw yourselves upon the foe, spill his blood; take to your wings and surround them on all sides. Woe to them! let us get to work with our beaks, let us devour them. Nothing can save them from our wrath, neither the mountain forests, nor the clouds that float in the sky, nor the foaming deep.

LEADER OF THE CHORUS: Come, peck, tear to ribbons. Where is the chief of the cohort? Let him engage the right wing.
(They rush at the two Athenians.)

EUELPIDES: This is the fatal moment. Where shall I fly to, unfortunate wretch that am?

PITHETAERUS: Wait! Stay here!

EUELPIDES: That they may tear me to pieces?

193

PITHETAERUS: And how do you think to escape them?

EUELPIDES: I don't know at all.

PITHETAERUS: Come, I will tell you. We must stop and fight them. Let us arm ourselves with these stew-pots.

EUELPIDES: Why with the stew-pots?

PITHETAERUS: The owl will not attack us then.

EUELPIDES: But do you see all those hooked claws?

PITHETAERUS: Take the spit and pierce the foe on your side.

EUELPIDES: And how about my eyes?

PITHETAERUS: Protect them with this dish or this vinegar-pot.

EUELPIDES: Oh! what cleverness! what inventive genius! You are a great general, even greater than Nicias, where stratagem is concerned.

LEADER OF THE CHORUS: Forward, forward, charge with your beaks! Come, no delay. Tear, pluck, strike, flay them, and first of all smash the stew-pot.

EPOPS: (stepping in front of the CHORUS:) Oh, most cruel of all animals, why tear these two men to pieces, why kill them? What have they done to you? They belong to the same tribe, to the same family as my wife.

LEADER OF THE CHORUS: Are wolves to be spared? Are they not our most mortal foes? So let us punish them.

EPOPS: If they are your foes by nature, they are your friends in heart, and they come here to give you useful advice.

194

LEADER OF THE CHORUS: Advice or a useful word from their lips, from them, the enemies of my forebears?

EPOPS: The wise can often profit by the lessons of a foe, for caution is the mother of safety. It is just such a thing as one will not learn from a friend and which an enemy compels you to know. To begin with, it's the foe and not the friend that taught cities to build high walls, to equip long vessels of war; and it's this knowledge that protects our children, our slaves and our wealth.

LEADER OF THE CHORUS: Well then, I agree, let us first hear them, for that is best; one can even learn something in an enemy's school.

PITHETAERUS: (to EUELPIDES) Their wrath seems to cool. Draw back a little.

EPOPS: It's only justice, and you will thank me later.

LEADER OF THE CHORUS: Never have we opposed your advice up to now.

PITHETAERUS: They are in a more peaceful mood,-put down your stew-pot and your two dishes; spit in hand, doing duty for a spear, let us mount guard inside the camp close to the pot and watch in our arsenal closely; for we must not fly.

EUELPIDES: You are right. But where shall we be buried, if we die?

PITHETAERUS: In the Ceramicus; for, to get a public funeral, we shall tell the Strategi that we fell at Orneae, fighting the country's foes.

LEADER OF THE CHORUS: Return to your ranks and lay down your courage beside your wrath as the hoplites do. Then let us ask these men who they are, whence they come, and with what intent. Here, Epops, answer me.

EPOPS: Are you calling me? What do you want of me?

LEADER OF THE CHORUS: Who are they? From what country?

195

EPOPS: Strangers, who have come from Greece, the land of the wise.

LEADER OF THE CHORUS: And what fate has led them hither to the land of the birds?

EPOPS: Their love for you and their wish to share your kind of life; to dwell and remain with you always.

LEADER OF THE CHORUS: Indeed, and what are their plans?

EPOPS: They are wonderful, incredible, unheard of.

LEADER OF THE CHORUS: Why, do they think to see some advantage that determines them to settle here? Are they hoping with our help to triumph over their foes or to be useful to their friends?

EPOPS: They speak of benefits so great it is impossible either to describe or conceive them; all shall be yours, all that we see here, there, above and below us; this they vouch for.

LEADER OF THE CHORUS: Are they mad?

EPOPS: They are the sanest people in the world.

LEADER OF THE CHORUS: Clever men?

EPOPS: The slyest of foxes, cleverness its very self, men of the world, cunning, the cream of knowing folk.

LEADER OF THE CHORUS: Tell them to speak and speak quickly; why, as I listen to you, I am beside myself with delight.

EPOPS: (to two attendants) Here, you there, take all these weapons and hang them up inside dose to the fire, near the figure of the god who presides there and

196

under his protection; (to PITHETAERUS) as for you, address the birds, tell them why I have gathered them together.

PITHETAERUS: Not I, by Apollo, unless they agree with me as the little ape of an armourer agreed with his wife, not to bite me, nor pull me by the balls, nor shove things into my...

EUELPIDES: (bending over and pointing his finger at his anus) Do you mean this?

PITHETAERUS: No, I mean my eyes.

LEADER OF THE CHORUS: Agreed.

PITHETAERUS: Swear it.

LEADER OF THE CHORUS: I swear it and, if I keep my promise, let judges and spectators give me the victory unanimously.

PITHETAERUS: It is a bargain.

LEADER OF THE CHORUS: And if I break my word, may I succeed by one vote only.

EPOPS: (as HERALD)   Hearken, ye people! Hoplites, pick up your weapons and return to your firesides; do not fail to read the decrees of dismissal we have posted.

CHORUS: (singing) Man is a truly cunning creature, but nevertheless explain. Perhaps you are going to show me some good way to extend my power, some way that I have not had the wit to find out and which you have discovered. Speak! 'tis to your own interest as well as to mine, for if you secure me some advantage, I will surely share it with you.

LEADER OF THE CHORUS: But what object can have induced you to come among us? Speak boldly, for I shall not break the truce,-until you have told us all.

PITHETAERUS: I am bursting with desire to speak; I have already mixed the dough of my address and nothing prevents me from kneading it....Slave! bring the chaplet and water, which you must pour over my hands. Be quick!

EUELPIDES: Is it a question of feasting? What does it all mean?

PITHETAERUS: By Zeus, no! but I am hunting for fine, tasty words to break down the hardness of their hearts. (To the CHORUS:) I grieve so much for you, who at one time were
kings...

LEADER OF THE CHORUS: We kings? Over whom?

PITHETAERUS: ...of all that exists, firstly of me and of this man, even of Zeus himself. Your race is older than Saturn, the
Titans and the Earth.

LEADER OF THE CHORUS: What, older than the Earth!

PITHETAERUS: By Phoebus, yes.

LEADER OF THE CHORUS: By Zeus, but I never knew that before!

PITHETAERUS: That's because you are ignorant and heedless, and have never read your Aesop. He is the one who tells us that the lark was born before all other creatures, indeed before the Earth; his father died of sickness, but the Earth did not exist then; he remained unburied for five days, when the bird in its dilemma decided, for want of a better place, to entomb its father in its own head.

EUELPIDES: So that the lark's father is buried at Cephalae.

PITHETAERUS: Hence, if they existed before the Earth, before the gods, the kingship belongs to them by right of priority.

EUELPIDES: Undoubtedly, but sharpen your beak well; Zeus won't be in a hurry to hand over his sceptre to the woodpecker.

PITHETAERUS: It was not the gods, but the birds, who were formerly the masters and kings over men; of this I have a thousand proofs. First of all, I will point you to the cock, who governed the Persians before all other monarchs, before Darius and Megabazus. It's in memory of his reign that he is called the Persian bird.

EUELPIDES: For this reason also, even to-day, he alone of all the birds wears his tiara straight on his head, like the Great King.

PITHETAERUS: He was so strong, so great, so feared, that even now, on account of his ancient power, everyone jumps out of bed as soon as ever he crows at daybreak. Blacksmiths, potters, tanners, shoemakers, bathmen, corndealers, lyre-makers and armourers, all put on their shoes and go to work before it is daylight.

EUELPIDES: I can tell you something about that. It was the cock's fault that I lost a splendid tunic of Phrygian wool. I was at a feast in town, given to celebrate the birth of a child; I had drunk pretty freely and had just fallen asleep, when a cock, I suppose in a greater hurry than the rest, began to crow. I thought it was dawn and set out for Halimus. I had hardly got beyond the walls, when a footpad struck me in the back with his bludgeon; down I went and wanted to shout, but he had already made off with my mantle.

PITHETAERUS: Formerly also thekite was ruler and king over the Greeks.

LEADER OF THE CHORUS: The Greeks?

PITHETAERUS: And when he was king, he was the one who first taught them to fall on their knees before the kites.

EUELPIDES: By Zeus! that's what I did myself one day on seeing a kite; but at the moment I was on my knees, and leaning backwards with mouth agape, I bolted an obolus and was forced to carry my meal-sack home empty.

PITHETAERUS: The cuckoo was king of Egypt and of the whole of Phoenicia. When he called out "cuckoo," all the Phoenicians hurried to the fields to reap their wheat and their barley.

EUELPIDES: Hence no doubt the proverb, "Cuckoo! cuckoo! go to the fields, ye circumcised."

PITHETAERUS: So powerful were the birds that the kings of Grecian cities, Agamemnon, Menelaus, for instance, carried A BIRD: on the tip of their sceptres, who had his share of all presents.

EUELPIDES: That I didn't know and was much astonished when I saw Priam come upon the stage in the tragedies with a bird, which kept watching Lysicrates to see if he got any present.

PITHETAERUS: But the strongest proof of all is that Zeus, who now reigns, is represented as standing with an eagle on his head as a symbol of his royalty; his daughter has an owl, and Phoebus, as his servant, has a hawk.

EUELPIDES: By Demeter, the point is well taken. But what are all these birds doing in heaven?

PITHETAERUS: When anyone sacrifices and, according to the rite, offers the entrails to the gods, these birds take their share before Zeus. Formerly men always swore by the birds and never by the gods.

EUELPIDES: And even now Lampon swears by the goose whenever he wishes to deceive someone.

PITHETAERUS: Thus it is clear that you were once great and sacred, but now you are looked upon as slaves, as fools, as Maneses; stones are thrown at you as at raving madmen, even in holy places. A crowd of bird-catchers sets snares, traps, limed twigs and nets of all sorts for you; you are caught, you are sold in heaps and the buyers finger you over to be certain you are fat. Again, if they would but serve you up simply roasted; but they rasp cheese into a mixture of oil, vinegar and laserwort, to which another sweet and greasy sauce is added, and the whole is poured scalding hot over your back, for all the world as if you were diseased meat.

CHORUS: (singing) Man, your words have made my heart bleed; I have groaned over the treachery of our fathers, who knew not how to transmit to us the high rank they held from their forefathers. But 'tis a benevolent Genius, a happy Fate, that sends you to us; you shall be our deliverer and I place the destiny of my little ones and my own in your hands with every confidence.

LEADER OF THE CHORUS: But hasten to tell me what must be done; we should not be worthy to live, if we did not seek to regain our royalty by every possible means.

PITHETAERUS: First I advise that the birds gather together in one city and that they build a wall of great bricks, like that at Babylon, round the plains of the air and the whole region of space that divides earth from heaven.

EPOPS: Oh, Cebriones! oh, Porphyrion! what a terribly strong place!

PITHETAERUS: Then, when this has been well done and completed, you demand back the empire from Zeus; if he will not agree, if he refuses and does not at once confess himself beaten, you declare a sacred war against him and forbid the gods henceforward to pass through your country with their tools up, as hitherto, for the purpose of laying their Alcmenas, their Alopes, or their Semeles! if they try to pass through, you put rings on their tools so that they can't make love any longer. You send another messenger to mankind, who will proclaim to them that the birds are kings, that for the future they must first of all sacrifice to them, and only afterwards to the gods; that it is fitting to appoint to each deity the bird that has most in common with it. For instance, are they sacrificing to Aphrodite, let them at the same time offer barley to the coot; are they immolating a sheep to Posidon, let them consecrate wheat in honour of the duck; if a steer is being offered to Heracles, let honey-cakes be dedicated to the

201

gull; if a goat is being slain for King Zeus, there is a King-Bird, the wren, to whom the sacrifice of a male gnat is due before Zeus himself even.

EUELPIDES: This notion of an immolated gnat delights me! And now let the great Zeus thunder!

LEADER OF THE CHORUS: But how will mankind recognize us as gods and not as jays? Us, who have wings and fly?

PITHETAERUS: You talk rubbish! Hermes is a god and has wings and flies, and so do many other gods. First of all, Victory flies with golden wings, Eros is undoubtedly winged too, and Iris is compared by Homer to a timorous dove.

EUELPIDES: But will not Zeus thunder and send his winged bolts against us?

LEADER OF THE CHORUS: If men in their blindness do not recognize us as gods and so continue to worship the dwellers in Olympus?

PITHETAERUS: Then a cloud of sparrows greedy for corn must descend upon their fields and eat up all their seeds; we shall see then if Demeter will mete them out any wheat.

EUELPIDES: By Zeus, she'll take good care she does not, and you will see her inventing a thousand excuses.

PITHETAERUS: The crows too will prove your divinity to them by pecking out the eyes of their flocks and of their draught-oxen; and then let Apollo cure them, since he is a physician and is paid for the purpose.

EUELPIDES: Oh! don't do that! Wait first until I have sold my two young bullocks.

PITHETAERUS: If on the other hand they recognize that you are God, the principle of life, that. you are Earth, Saturn, Posidon, they shall be loaded with benefits.

LEADER OF THE CHORUS: Name me one of these then.

PITHETAERUS: Firstly, the locusts shall not eat up their vine-blossoms; a legion of owls and kestrels will devour them. Moreover, the gnats and the gallbugs shall no longer ravage the figs; a flock of thrushes shall swallow the whole host down to the very last.

LEADER OF THE CHORUS: And how shall we give wealth to mankind? This is their strongest passion.

PITHETAERUS: When they consult the omens, you will point them to the richest mines, you will reveal the paying ventures to the diviner, and not another shipwreck will happen or sailor perish.

LEADER OF THE CHORUS: No more shall perish? How is that?

PITHETAERUS: When the auguries are examined before starting on a voyage, some bird will not fail to say, "Don't start! there will be a storm," or else, "Go! you will make a most profitable venture."

EUELPIDES: I shall buy a trading-vessel and go to sea, I will not stay with you.

PITHETAERUS: You will discover treasures to them, which were buried in former times, for you know them. Do not all men say, "None knows where my treasure lies, unless perchance it be some bird."

EUELPIDES: I shall sell my boat and buy a spade to unearth the vessels.

LEADER OF THE CHORUS: And how are we to give them health, which belongs to the gods?

PITHETAERUS: If they are happy, is not that the chief thing towards health? The miserable man is never well.

LEADER OF THE CHORUS: Old Age also dwells in Olympus. How will they get at it? Must they die in early youth?

PITHETAERUS: Why, the birds, by Zeus, will add three hundred years to their life.

LEADER OF THE CHORUS: From whom will they take them?

PITHETAERUS: From whom? Why, from themselves. Don't you know the cawing crow lives five times as long as a man?

EUELPIDES: Ah! ah! these are far better kings for us than Zeus!

PITHETAERUS: (solemnly) Far better, are they not? And firstly, we shall not have to build them temples of hewn stone, closed with gates of gold; they will dwell amongst the bushes and in the thickets of green oak; the most venerated of birds will have no other temple than the foliage of the olive tree; we shall not go to Delphi or to Ammon to sacrifice; but standing erect in the midst of arbutus and wild olives and holding forth our hands filled with wheat and barley, we shall pray them to admit us to a share of the blessings they enjoy and shall at once obtain them for a few grains of wheat.

LEADER OF THE CHORUS: Old man, whom I detested, you are now to me the dearest of all; never shall I, if I can help it, fail to follow your advice.

CHORUS: (singing) Inspirited by your words, I threaten my rivals the gods, and I swear that if you march in alliance with me against the gods and are faithful to our just, loyal and sacred bond, we shall soon have shattered their sceptre,

LEADER OF THE CHORUS: We shall charge ourselves with the performance of everything that requires force; that which demands thought and deliberation shall be yours to supply.

EPOPS By Zeus! it's no longer the time to delay and loiter like Nicias; let us act as promptly as possible.... In the first place, come, enter my nest built of brushwood and blades of straw, and tell me your names.

PITHETAERUS: That is soon done; my name is Pithetaerus, and his, Euelpides, of the deme Crioa.

EPOPS: Good! and good luck to you.

PITHETAERUS: We accept the omen.

EPOPS: Come in here.

PITHETAERUS: Very well, you are the one who must lead us and introduce us.

EPOPS: Come then. (He starts to fly away.)

PITHETAERUS: (stopping himself) Oh! my god! do come back here. Hi! tell us how we are to follow you. You can fly, but we cannot.

EPOPS: Well, well.

PITHETAERUS: Remember Aesop's fables. It is told there that the fox fared very badly, because he had made an alliance with the eagle.

EPOPS: Be at ease. You shall eat a certain root and wings will grow on your shoulders.

PITHETAERUS: Then let us enter.

XANTHIAS: and Manodorus, pick up our baggage.

LEADER OF THE CHORUS: Hi! Epops! do you hear me?

EPOPS: What's the matter?

LEADER OF THE CHORUS: Take them off to dine well and call your mate, the melodious Procne, whose songs are worthy of the Muses; she will delight our leisure moments.

PITHETAERUS: Oh! I conjure you, accede to their wish; for this delightful bird will leave her rushes at the sound of your voice; for the sake of the gods, let her come here, so that we may contemplate the nightingale.

EPOPS: Let is be as you desire. Come forth, Procne, show yourself to these strangers.

(PROCNE appears; she resembles a young flute-girl.)

PITHETAERUS: Oh! great Zeus! what a beautiful little bird! what a dainty form! what brilliant plumage! Do you know how dearly I should like to get between her thighs?

EUELPIDES: She is dazzling all over with gold, like a young girl. Oh! how I should like to kiss her!

PITHETAERUS: Why, wretched man, she has two little sharp points on her beak!

EUELPIDES: I would treat her like an egg, the shell of which we remove before eating it; I would take off her mask and then kiss her pretty face.

EPOPS: Let us go in.

PITHETAERUS: Lead the way, and may success attend us.

(EPOPS goes into the thicket, followed by PITHETAERUS and EUELPIDES.)

CHORUS: (singing) Lovable golden bird, whom I cherish above all others, you, whom I associate with all my songs, nightingale, you have come, you have come, to show yourself to me and to charm me with your notes. Come, you, who play spring melodies upon the harmonious flute, lead off our anapests. (The CHORUS: turns and faces the audience.)

LEADER OF THE CHORUS: Weak mortals, chained to the earth, creatures of clay as frail as the foliage of the woods, you unfortunate race, whose life is but

206

darkness, as unreal as a shadow, the illusion of a dream, hearken to us, who are immortal beings, ethereal, ever young and occupied with eternal thoughts, for we shall teach you about all celestial matters; you shall know thoroughly what is the nature of the birds, what the origin of the gods, of the rivers, of Erebus, and Chaos; thanks to us, even Prodicus will envy you your knowledge. At the beginning there was only Chaos, Night, dark Erebus, and deep Tartarus. Earth, the air and heaven had no existence. Firstly, black-winged Night laid a germless egg in the bosom of the infinite deeps of Erebus, and from this, after the revolution of long ages, sprang the graceful Eros with his glittering golden wings, swift as the whirlwinds of the tempest. He mated in deep Tartarus with dark Chaos, winged like himself, and thus hatched forth our race, which was the first to see the light. That of the Immortals did not exist until Eros had brought together all the ingredients of the world, and from their marriage Heaven, Ocean, Earth and the imperishable race of blessed gods sprang into being. Thus our origin is very much older than that of the dwellers in Olympus. We are the offspring of Eros; there are a thousand proofs to show it. We have wings and we lend assistance to lovers. How many handsome youths, who had sworn to remain insensible, have opened their thighs because of our power and have yielded themselves to their lovers when almost at the end of their youth, being led away by the gift of a quail, a waterfowl, a goose, or a cock. And what important services do not the birds render to mortals! First of all, they mark the seasons for them, springtime, winter, and autumn. Does the screaming crane migrate to Libya,-it warns the husbandman to sow, the pilot to take his ease beside his tiller hung up in his dwelling, and Orestes to weave a tunic, so that the rigorous cold may not drive him any more to strip other folk. When the kite reappears, he tells of the return of spring and of the period when the fleece of the sheep must be clipped. Is the swallow in sight? All hasten to sell their warm tunic and to buy some light clothing. We are your Ammon, Delphi, Dodona, your Phoebus Apollo. Before undertaking anything, whether a business transaction, a marriage, or the purchase of food, you consult the birds by reading the omens, and you give this name of omen to all signs that tell of the future. With you a word is an omen, you call a sneeze an omen, a meeting an omen, an unknown sound an omen, a slave or an ass an omen. Is it not clear that we are a prophetic Apollo to you? (More and more rapidly from here on.) If you recognize us as gods, we shall be your divining Muses, through us you will know the winds and the seasons, summer, winter, and the temperate months. We

207

shall not withdraw ourselves to the highest clouds like Zeus, but shall be among you and shall give to you and to your children and the children of your children, health and wealth, long life, peace, youth, laughter, songs and feasts; in short, you will all be so well off, that you will be weary and cloyed with enjoyment.

FIRST SEMI-CHORUS: (singing) Oh, rustic Muse of such varied note, tiotiotiotiotiotinx, I sing with you in the groves and on the mountain tops, tiotiotiotinx. I poured forth sacred strains from my golden throat in honour of the god Pan, tiotiotiotinx, from the top of the thickly leaved ash, and my voice mingles with the mighty choirs who extol Cybele on the mountain tops, totototototototototinx. 'Tis to our concerts that Phrynichus comes to pillage like a bee the ambrosia of his songs, the sweetness of which so charms the ear, tiotiotiotinx.

LEADER OF FIRST SEMI-CHORUS: If there is one of you spectators who wishes to spend the rest of his life quietly among the birds, let him come to us. All that is disgraceful and forbidden by law on earth is on the contrary honourable among us, the birds. For instance, among you it's a crime to beat your father, but with us it's an estimable deed; it's considered fine to run straight at your father and hit him, saying, "Come, lift your spur if you want to fight." The runaway slave, whom you brand, is only a spotted francolin with us. Are you Phrygian like Spintharus? Among us you would be the Phrygian bird, the goldfinch, of the race of Philemon. Are you a slave and a Carian like Execestides? Among us you can create yourself fore-fathers; you can always find relations. Does the son of Pisias want to betray the gates of the city to the foe? Let him become a partridge, the fitting offspring of his father; among us there is no shame in escaping as cleverly as a partridge.

SECOND SEMI-CHORUS: (singing) So the swans on the banks of the Hebrus, tiotiotiotiotinx, mingle their voices to serenade Apollo, tiotiotiotinx, flapping their wings the while, tiotiotiotinx; their notes reach beyond the clouds of heaven; they startle the various tribes of the beasts; a windles sky calms the waves, totototototototototinx; all Olympus resounds, and astonishment seizes its rulers; the Olympian graces and Muses cry aloud the strain, tiotiotiotinx.

LEADER OF SECOND SEMI-CHORUS: There is nothing more useful nor more pleasant than to have wings. To begin with, just let us suppose a spectator to be dying with hunger and to be weary of the choruses of the tragic poets; if he were winged, he would fly off, go home to dine and come back with his stomach filled. Some Patroclides, needing to take a crap, would not have to spill it out on his cloak, but could fly off, satisfy his requirements, let a few farts and, having recovered his breath, return. If one of you, it matters not who, had adulterous relations and saw the husband of his mistress in the seats of the senators, he might stretch his wings, fly to her, and, having laid her, resume his place. Is it not the most priceless gift of all, to be winged? Look at Diitrephes! His wings were only wicker-work ones, and yet he got himself chosen Phylarch and then Hipparch; from being nobody, he has risen to be famous; he's now the finest gilded cock of his tribe.

(PITHETAERUS and EUELPIDES return; they now have wings.)

PITHETAERUS: Halloa! What's this? By Zeus! I never saw anything so funny in all my life.

EUELPIDES: What makes you laugh?

PITHETAERUS: Your little wings. D'you know what you look like? Like a goose painted by some dauber.

EUELPIDES: And you look like a close-shaven blackbird.

PITHETAERUS: We ourselves asked for this transformation, and, as Aeschylus has it, "These are no borrowed feathers, but truly our own."

EPOPS: Come now, what must be done?

PITHETAERUS: First give our city a great and famous name, then sacrifice to the gods.

EUELPIDES: I think so too.

LEADER OF THE CHORUS: Let's see. What shall our city be called?

PITHETAERUS: Will you have a high-sounding Laconian name? Shall we call it Sparta?

EUELPIDES: What! call my town Sparta? Why, I would not use esparto for my bed, even though I had nothing but bands of rushes.

PITHETAERUS: Well then, what name can you suggest?

EUELPIDES: Some name borrowed from the clouds, from these lofty regions in which we dwell-in short, some well-known name.

PITHETAERUS: Do you like Nephelococcygia?

LEADER OF THE CHORUS: Oh! capital! truly that's a brilliant thought!

EUELPIDES: Is it in Nephelococcygia that all the wealth of Theogenes and most of Aeschines' is?

PITHETAERUS: No, it's rather the plain of Phlegra, where the gods withered the pride of the sons of the Earth with their shafts.

LEADER OF THE CHORUS: Oh! what a splendid city! But what god shall be its patron? for whom shall we weave the peplus?

EUELPIDES: Why not choose Athene Polias?

PITHETAERUS: Oh! what a well-ordered town it would be to have a female deity armed from head to foot, while Clisthenes was spinning!

LEADER OF THE CHORUS: Who then shall guard the Pelargicon?

PITHETAERUS: A Bird.

LEADER OF THE CHORUS: One of us? What kind of bird?

PITHETAERUS: A Bird of Persian strain, who is everywhere proclaimed to be the bravest of all, a true chick of Ares.

EUELPIDES: Oh! noble chick!

PITHETAERUS: Because he is a god well suited to live on the rocks. Come! into the air with you to help the workers who are building the wall; carry up rubble, strip yourself to mix the mortar, take up the hod, tumble down the ladder, if you like, post sentinels, keep the fire smouldering beneath the ashes, go round the walls, bell in hand, and go to sleep up there yourself then despatch two heralds, one to the gods above, the other to mankind on earth and come back here.

EUELPIDES: As for yourself, remain here, and may the plague take you for a troublesome fellow! (He departs.)

PITHETAERUS: Go, friend, go where I send you, for without you my orders cannot be obeyed. For myself, I want to sacrifice to the new god, and I am going to summon the Priest who must preside at the ceremony. Slaves! slaves! bring forward the basket and the lustral water.

CHORUS: (singing) I do as you do, and I wish as you wish, and I implore you to address powerful and solemn prayers to the gods, and in addition to immolate a sheep as a token of our gratitude. Let us sing the Pythian chant in honour of the god, and let Chaeris accompany our voices.

PITHETAERUS: Enough! but, by Heracles! what is this? Great gods! I have seen many prodigious things, but I never saw a muzzled raven. (The PRIEST arrives.)

PRIEST: It's high time! Sacrifice to the new gods.

PRIEST: I begin, but where is the man with the basket? Pray to the Hestia of the birds, to the kite, who presides over the hearth, and to all the god and goddess-birds who dwell in Olympus...

PITHETAERUS: Oh! Hawk, the sacred guardian of Sunium, oh, god of the storks!

PRIEST: ...to the swan of Delos, to Leto the mother of the quails, and to Artemis, the goldfinch...

PITHETAERUS: It's no longer Artemis Colaenis, but Artemis the goldfinch.

PRIEST: ...to Bacchus, the finch and Cybele, the ostrich and mother of the gods and mankind...

PITHETAERUS: Oh! sovereign ostrich Cybele, mother of Cleocritus!

PRIEST: ...to grant health and safety to the Nephelococcygians as well as to the dwellers in Chios...

PITHETAERUS: The dwellers in Chios! Ah! I am delighted they should be thus mentioned on all occasions.

PRIEST: ...to the heroes, the birds, to the sons of heroes, to the porphyrion, the pelican, the spoon-bill, the redbreast, the grouse, the peacock, the horned-owl, the teal, the bittern, the heron, the stormy petrel, the fig-pecker, the titmouse...

PITHETAERUS: Stop! stop! you drive me crazy with your
endless list. Why, wretch, to what sacred feast are you inviting the vultures and the sea-eagles? Don't you see that a single kite could easily carry off the lot at once? Begone, you and your fillets and all; I shall know how to complete the sacrifice by myself.

(The PRIEST departs.)

It is imperative that I sing another sacred chant for the rite of the lustral water, and that I invoke the immortals, or at least one of them, provided always that

212

you have some suitable food to offer him; from what I see here, in the shape of gifts, there is naught whatever but horn and hair.

PITHETAERUS: Let us address our sacrifices and our prayers to the winged gods.

(A POET: enters.)

POET: Oh, Muse! celebrate happy Nephelococcygia in your hymns.

PITHETAERUS: What have we here? Where did you come from, tell me? Who are you?

POET: I am he whose language is sweeter than honey, the zealous slave of the Muses, as Homer has it.

PITHETAERUS: You a slave! and yet you wear your hair long?

POET: No, but the fact is all we poets are the assiduous slaves of the Muses, according to Homer.

PITHETAERUS: In truth your little cloak is quite holy too through zeal! But, poet, what ill wind drove you here?

POET: I have composed verses in honour of your Nephelococcygia, a host of splendid dithyrambs and parthenia worthy of Simonides himself.

PITHETAERUS: And when did you compose them? How long since?

POET: Oh! 'tis long, aye, very long, that I have sung in honour of this city.

PITHETAERUS: But I am only celebrating its foundation with this sacrifice; I have only just named it, as is done with little babies.

POET: "Just as the chargers fly with the speed of the wind, so does the voice of the Muses take its flight. Oh! thou noble founder of the town of Aetna, thou, whose name recalls the holy sacrifices, make us such gift as thy generous heart shall suggest." (He puts out his hand.)

PITHETAERUS: He will drive us silly if we do not get rid of him by some present. (To the PRIEST'S acolyte) Here! you, who have a fur as well as your tunic, take it off and give it to this clever poet. Come, take this fur; you look to me to be shivering with cold.

POET: My Muse will gladly accept this gift; but engrave these verses of Pindar's on your mind.

PITHETAERUS: Oh! what a pest! It's impossible then to get rid of him!

POET: "Straton wanders among the Scythian nomads, but has no linen garment. He is sad at only wearing an animal's pelt and no tunic." Do you get what I mean?

PITHETAERUS: I understand that you want me to offer you a tunic. Hi! you (to the acolyte), take off yours; we must help the Poet ....Come, you, take it and get out.

POET: I am going, and these are the verses that I address to this city: "Phoebus of the golden throne, celebrate this shivery, freezing city; I have travelled through fruitful and snow-covered plains. Tralala! Tralala!" (He departs.)

PITHETAERUS: What are you chanting us about frosts? Thanks to the tunic, you no longer fear them. Ah! by Zeus! I could not have believed this cursed fellow could so soon have learnt the way to our city. (To a slave) Come, take the lustral water and circle the altar. Let all keep silence!

(An ORACLE-MONGER enters.)

ORACLE-MONGER: Let not the goat be sacrificed.

PITHETAERUS: Who are you?

ORACLE-MONGER: Who am I? An Oracle-Monger .

PITHETAERUS: Get out!

ORACLE-MONGER: Wretched man, insult not sacred things. For there is an oracle of Bacis, which exactly applies to Nephelococcygia.

PITHETAERUS: Why did you not reveal it to me before I founded my city?

ORACLE-MONGER: The divine spirit was against it.

PITHETAERUS: Well, I suppose there's nothing to do but hear the terms of the oracle.

ORACLE-MONGER: "But when the wolves and the white crows shall dwell together between Corinth and Sicyon..."

PITHETAERUS: But how do the Corinthians concern me?

ORACLE-MONGER: It is the regions of the air that Bacis indicates in this manner. "They must first sacrifice a white-fleeced goat to Pandora, and give the prophet who first reveals my words a good cloak and new sandals."

PITHETAERUS: Does it say sandals there?

ORACLE-MONGER: Look at the book. "And besides this a goblet of wine and a good share of the entrails of the entrails of the victim."

PITHETAERUS: Of the entrails-does it say that?

ORACLE-MONGER: Look at the book. "If you do as I command, divine youth, you shall be an eagle among the clouds; if not, you shall be neither turtle-dove, nor eagle, nor woodpecker."

PITHETAERUS: Does it say all that?

ORACLE-MONGER: Look at the book.

PITHETAERUS: Thisoracle in no sort of way resembles the one Apollo dictated to me: "If an impostor comes without invitation to annoy you during the sacrifice and to demand a share of the victim, apply a stout stick to his ribs."

ORACLE-MONGER: You are drivelling.

PITHETAERUS: Look at the book. "And don't spare him, were he an eagle from out of the clouds, were it Lampon himself or the great Diopithes."

ORACLE-MONGER: Does it say that?

PITHETAERUS: Look at the book and go and hang yourself.

ORACLE-MONGER: Oh! unfortunate wretch that I am. (He departs.)

PITHETAERUS: Away with you, and take your prophecies elsewhere.

(Enter METON, With surveying instruments.)

METON: I have come to you...

PITHETAERUS: (interrupting) Yet another pest! What have you come to do? What's your plan?   What's the purpose of your journey? Why these splendid buskins?

METON: I want to survey the plains of the air for you and to parcel them into lots.

PITHETAERUS: In the name of the gods, who are you?

METON: Who am I? Meton, known throughout Greece and at Colonus.

PITHETAERUS: What are these things?

216

METON: Tools for measuring the air. In truth, the spaces in the air have precisely the form of a furnace. With this bent ruler I draw a line from top to bottom; from one of its points I describe a circle with the compass. Do you understand?

PITHETAERUS: Not in the least.

METON: With the straight ruler I set to work to inscribe a square within this circle; in its centre will be the market-place, into which all the straight streets will lead, converging to this centre like a star, which, although only orbicular, sends forth its rays in a straight line from all sides.

PITHETAERUS: A regular Thales! Meton ...

METON: What d'you want with me?

PITHETAERUS: I want to give you a proof of my friendship. Use your legs.

METON: Why, what have I to fear?

PITHETAERUS: It's the same here as in Sparta. Strangers are driven away, and blows rain down as thick as hail.
METON: Is there sedition in your city?

PITHETAERUS: No,certainly not.

METON: What's wrong then?

PITHETAERUS: We are agreed to sweep all quacks and impostors far from our borders.

METON: Then I'll be going.

PITHETAERUS: I'm afraid it's too late. The thunder growls already. (He beats him.)

METON: Oh, woe! oh, woe!

PITHETAERUS: I warned you. Now, be off, and do your surveying somewhere else.

(METON   takes to his heels. He is no sooner gone than an INSPECTOR arrives.)

INSPECTOR: Where are the Proxeni?

PITHETAERUS: Who is this Sardanapalus?

INSPECTOR: I have been appointed by lot to come to Nephelococcygia. as Inspector.

PITHETAERUS: An Inspector! and who sends you here, you rascal?

INSPECTOR: A decree of Teleas.

PITHETAERUS: Will you just pocket your salary, do nothing, and get out?

INSPECTOR: Indeed I will; I am urgently needed to be at Athens to attend the Assembly; for I am charged with the interests of Pharnaces.

PITHETAERUS: Take it then, and get on your way. This is your salary. (He beats him.)

INSPECTOR: What does this mean?

PITHETAERUS: This is the assembly where you have to defend Pharnaces.

INSPECTOR: You shall testify that they dare to strike me, the Inspector.

PITHETAERUS: Are you not going to get out with your urns? It's not to be believed; they send us Inspectors before we have so much as paid sacrifice to the gods.

(The INSPECTOR goes into hiding. A DEALER IN DECREES arrives.)

DEALER IN DECREES: (reading) "If the Nephelococcygian does wrong to the Athenian..."

PITHETAERUS: What trouble now? What book is that?

DEALER IN DECREES: I am a dealer in decrees, and I have come here to sell you the new laws.

PITHETAERUS: Which?

DEALER IN DECREES   "The Nephelococcygians shall adopt the same weights, measures and decrees as the Olophyxians."

PITHETAERUS: And you shall soon be imitating the Ototyxians. (He beats him.)

DEALER IN DECREES: Ow! what are you doing?

PITHETAERUS: Now will you get out of here with your decrees? For I am going to let you see some severe ones.

(The DEALER IN DECREES departs; the INSPECTOR comes out of hiding.)

INSPECTOR: (returning) I summon Pithetaerus for outrage for the month of Munychion.

PITHETAERUS: Ha! my friend! are you still here?

(The DEALER IN DECREES also returns.)

DEALER IN DECREES: "Should anyone drive away the magistrates and not receive them, according to the decree duly posted..." Pithetaerus What! rascal! you are back too? (He rushes at him.)

INSPECTOR: Woe to you! I'll have you condemned to a fine of ten thousand drachmae.

PITHETAERUS: And I'll smash your urns.

INSPECTOR: Do you recall that evening when you crapped on the column where the decrees are posted?

PITHETAERUS: Here! here! let him be seized.

(The INSPECTOR runs off.)

Why, don't you want to stay any longer? But let us get indoors as quick as possible; we will sacrifice the goat inside.

FIRST SEMI-CHORUS: (singing) Henceforth it is to me that mortals must address their sacrifices and their prayers. Nothing escapes my sight nor my might My glance embraces the universe, I preserve the fruit in the flower by destroying the thousand kinds of voracious insects the soil produces, which attack the trees and feed on the germ when it has scarcely formed in the calyx; I destroy those who ravage the balmy terrace gardens like a deadly plague; all these gnawing crawling creatures perish beneath the lash of my wing.

LEADER OF FIRST SEMI-CHORUS: I hear it proclaimed everywhere: "A talent for him who shall kill Diagoras of Melos, and a talent for him who destroys one of the dead tyrants." We likewise wish to make our proclamation: "A talent to him among you who shall kill Philocrates, the Struthian; four, if he brings him to us alive. For this Philocrates skewers the finches together and sells them at the rate of an obolus for seven. He tortures the thrushes by blowing them out, so that they may look bigger, sticks their own feathers into the nostrils of blackbirds, and collects pigeons, which he shuts up and forces them, fastened in a net, to decoy others." That is what we wish to proclaim. And if anyone is

220

keeping birds shut up in his yard, let him hasten to let them loose; those who disobey shall be seized by the birds and we shall put them in chains, so that in their turn they may decoy other men.

SECOND SEMI-CHORUS: (singing) Happy indeed is the race of winged birds who need no cloak in winter! Neither do I fear the relentless rays of the fiery dog-days; when the divine grasshopper, intoxicated with the sunlight, as noon is burning the ground, is breaking out into shrill melody; my home is beneath the foliage in the flowery meadows. I winter in deep caverns, where I frolic with the mountain nymphs, while in spring I despoil the gardens of the Graces and gather the white, virgin berry on the myrtle bushes.

LEADER OF SECOND SEMI-CHORUS: I want now to speak to the judges about the prize they are going to award; if they are favourable to us, we will load them with benefits far greater than those Paris received. Firstly, the owls of Laurium, which every judge desires above all things, shall never be wanting to you; you shall see them homing with you, building their nests in your money-bags and laying coins. Besides, you shall be housed like the gods, for we shall erect gables over your dwellings; if you hold some public post and want to do a little pilfering, we will give you the sharp claws of a hawk. Are you dining in town, we will provide you with stomachs as capacious as a bird's crop. But, if your award is against us, don't fail to have metal covers fashioned for yourselves, like those they place over statues; else, look out! for the day you wear a white tunic all the birds will soil it with their droppings.

PITHETAERUS: Birds! the sacrifice is propitious. But I see no messenger coming from the wall to tell us what is happening. Ah! here comes one running himself out of breath as though he were in the Olympic stadium.

MESSENGER: (running back and forth) Where, where, where is he? Where, where, where is he? Where, where, where is he? Where is Pithetaerus, our leader?

PITHETAERUS: Here am I.

MESSENGER: The wall is finished.

PITHETAERUS: That's good news.

MESSENGER: It's a most beautiful, a most magnificent work of art. The wall is so broad that Proxenides, the Braggartian, and Theogenes could pass each other in their chariots, even if they were drawn by steeds as big as the Trojan horse.

PITHETAERUS: That's fine!

MESSENGER: Its length is one hundred stadia; I measured it myself.

PITHETAERUS: A decent length, by Posidon! And who built such a wall?

MESSENGER: Birds-Birds only; they had neither Egyptian brickmaker, nor stone-mason, nor carpenter; the birds   did it all themselves; I could   hardly believe my eyes. Thirty thousand cranes came from Libya with   a supply of stones, intended for the foundations. The water-rails chiselled them with their beaks. Ten thousand storks were busy making bricks; plovers and other water fowl carried water into the air.

PITHETAERUS: And who carried the mortar?

MESSENGER: Herons, in hods.

PITHETAERUS: But how could they put the mortar into the hods?

MESSENGER: Oh! it was a truly clever invention; the geese used their feet   like spades; they buried them in the pile of mortar and then emptied them into the hods.

PITHETAERUS: Ah! to what use cannot feet be put?

MESSENGER: You should have seen how eagerly the ducks carried bricks. To complete the tale, the swallows came flying to the work, their beaks   full of mortar and their trowels on their backs, just the way little children are carried.

222

PITHETAERUS: Who would want paid servants after this? But tell me, who did the woodwork?

MESSENGER: Birds again, aid clever carpenters too, the pelicans, for they squared up the gates with their beaks in such a fashion that one would have thought they were using axes; the noise was just like a dockyard. Now the whole wall is tight everywhere, securely bolted and well guarded; it is patrolled, bell in hand; the sentinels stand everywhere and beacons burn on the towers. But I must run off to clean myself; the rest is your
business. (He departs.)

LEADER OF THE CHORUS: (to PITHETAERUS:)   Well! what do you say to it? Are you not astonished at the wall being completed so quickly?

PITHETAERUS: By the gods, yes, and with good reason. It's really not to be believed. But here comes another messenger from the wall to bring us some further news! What a fighting look he has!

SECOND MESSENGER: (rushing in) Alas! alas! alas! alas! alas! alas!

PITHETAERUS: What's the matter?

SECOND MESSENGER: A horrible outrage has occurred; a god sent by Zeus has passed through our gates and has penetrated the realms of the air without the knowledge of the jays, who are on guard in the daytime.

PITHETAERUS: It's a terrible and criminal deed. What god was it?

SECOND MESSENGER: We don't know that. All we know is, that he has got wings.

PITHETAERUS: Why were not patrolmen sent against him at once?

SECOND MESSENGER: We have despatched thirty thousand hawks of the legion of Mounted Archers. All the hook-clawed birds are moving against him, the kestrel, the buzzard, the vulture, the great-horned owl; they cleave the air so

223

that it resounds with the flapping of their wings; they are looking everywhere for the god, who cannot be far away; indeed, if I mistake not, he is coming from yonder side.

PITHETAERUS: To arms, all, with slings and bows! This way, all our soldiers; shoot and strike! Some one give me a sling!

CHORUS: (singing) War, a terrible war is breaking out between us and the gods! Come, let each one guard Air, the son of Erebus, in which the clouds float. Take care no immortal enters it without your knowledge.

LEADER OF THE CHORUS: Scan all sides with your glance. Hark! methinks I can hear the rustle of the swift wings of a god from heaven.

(The Machine brings in IRIS, in the form of a young girl.)

PITHETAERUS: Hi! you woman! where, where, are you flying to? Halt, don't stir! keep motionless! not a beat of your wing! (She pauses in her flight.) Who are you and from what country? You must say whence you come.

IRIS: I come from the abode of the Olympian gods.

PITHETAERUS: What's your name, ship or head-dress?

IRIS: I am swift Iris.

PITHETAERUS: Paralus or Salaminia?

IRIS: What do you mean?

PITHETAERUS: Let a buzzard rush at her and seize her.

IRIS: Seize me? But what do all these insults mean?

PITHETAERUS: Woe to you!

IRIS: I do not understand it.

PITHETAERUS: By which gate did you pass through the wall, wretched woman?

IRIS: By which gate? Why, great gods, I don't know.

PITHETAERUS: You hear how she holds us in derision. Did you present yourself to the officers in command of the jays? You don't answer. Have you a permit, bearing the seal of the storks?

IRIS: Am I dreaming?

PITHETAERUS: Did you get one?

IRIS: Are you mad?

PITHETAERUS: No head-bird gave you a safe-conduct?

IRIS: A safe-conduct to me. You poor fool!

PITHETAERUS: Ah! and so you slipped into this city on the sly and into these realms of air-land that don't belong to you.

IRIS: And what other roads can the gods travel?

PITHETAERUS: By Zeus! I know nothing about that, not I. But they won't pass this way. And you still dare to complain? Why, if you were treated according to your deserts, no Iris would ever have more justly suffered death.

IRIS: I am immortal.

PITHETAERUS: You would have died nevertheless.-Oh! that would be truly intolerable! What! should the universe obey us and the gods alone continue their insolence and not understand that they must submit to the law of the strongest in their due turn? But tell me, where are you flying to?

225

IRIS: I? The messenger of Zeus to mankind, I am going to tell them to sacrifice sheep and oxen on the altars and to fill their streets with the rich smoke of burning fat.

PITHETAERUS: Of which gods are you speaking?

IRIS: Of which? Why, of ourselves, the gods of heaven.

PITHETAERUS: You, gods?

IRIS: Are there others then?

PITHETAERUS: Men now adore the birds as gods, and it's to them, by Zeus, that they must offer sacrifices, and not to Zeus at all!

IRIS: (in tragic style) Oh! fool! fool! fool! Rouse not the wrath of the gods, for it is terrible indeed. Armed with the brand of Zeus, justice would annihilate your race; the lightning would strike you as it did Licymnius and consume both your body and the porticos of your palace.

PITHETAERUS: Here! that's enough tall talk. Just you listen and keep quiet! Do you take me for a Lydian or a Phrygian and think to frighten me with your big words? Know, that if Zeus worries me again, I shall go at the head of my eagles, who are armed with lightning, and reduce his dwelling and that of Amphion to cinders. I shall send more than six hundred porphyrions clothed in leopards' skins up to heaven against him; and formerly a single Porphyrion gave him enough to do. As for you, his messenger, if you annoy me, I shall begin by getting between your thighs, and even though you are IRIS: , you will be surprised at the erection the old man can produce; it's three times as good as the ram on a ship's prow!

IRIS: May you perish, you wretch, you and your infamous words!

PITHETAERUS: Won't you get out of here quickly? Come, stretch your wings or look out for squalls!

226

IRIS: If my father does not punish you for your insults...

(The Machine takes IRIS: away.)

PITHETAERUS: Ha!... but just yoube off elsewhere to roast younger folk than us with your lightning.

CHORUS: (singing) We forbid the gods, the sons of Zeus, to pass through our city and the mortals to send them the smoke of their sacrifices by this road.

PITHETAERUS: It's odd that the messenger we sent to the mortals has never returned.

(The HERALD   enters, wearing agolden garland on his head.)

HERALD: Oh! blessed Pithetaerus, very wise, very illustrious, very gracious, thrice happy, very...Come, prompt me, somebody, do.

PITHETAERUS: Get to your story!

HERALD: All peoples are filled with admiration for your wisdom, and they award you this golden crown.

PITHETAERUS: I accept it. But tell me, why do the people admire me?

HERALD: Oh you, who have founded so illustrious a city in the air, you know not in what esteem men hold you and how many there are who burn with desire to dwell in it. Before your city was built, all men had a mania for Sparta; long hair and fasting were held in honour, men went dirty like Socrates and carried staves. Now all is changed. Firstly, as soon as it's dawn, they all spring out of bed together to go and seek their food, the same as you do; then they fly off towards the notices and finally devour the decrees. The bird-madness is so clear that many actually bear the names of birds. There is a halting victualler, who styles himself the partridge; Menippus calls himself the swallow; Opuntius the one-eyed crow; Philocles the lark; Theogenes the fox-goose; Lycurgus the ibis; Chaerephon the bat; Syracosius the magpie; Midias the quail; indeed he looks like a quail that has been hit hard on the head. Out of love for the birds they repeat all the songs which concern the swallow, the teal, the goose or the pigeon; in each verse you see wings, or at all events a few feathers. This is what is happening down there. Finally, there are more than ten thousand folk who are coming here from earth to ask you for feathers and hooked claws; so, mind you supply yourself with wings for the immigrants.

PITHETAERUS: Ah! by Zeus, there's no time for idling. (To some slaves) Go as quick as possible and fill every hamper, every basket you can find with wings. Manes will bring them to me outside the walls, where I will welcome those who present themselves.

CHORUS: (Singing) This town will soon be inhabited by a crowd of men. Fortune favours us alone and thus they have fallen in love with our city.

PITHETAERUS: (to the slave MANES, who brings in a basket full of wings) Come, hurry up and bring them along.

CHORUS: (singing) Will not man find here everything that can please him-wisdom, love, the divine Graces, the sweet face of gentle peace?

PITHETAERUS: (as MANES Comes in with another basket) Oh! you lazy servant! won't you hurry yourself?

CHORUS: (singing) Let a basket of wings be brought speedily. Come, beat him as I do, and put some life into him; he is as lazy as an ass.

PITHETAERUS: Aye, Manes is a great craven.

CHORUS: (singing) Begin by putting this heap of wings in order; divide them in three parts according to the birds from whom they came; the singing, the prophetic and the aquatic birds then you must take care to distribute them to the men according to their character.

PITHETAERUS: (to Manes, who is bringing in another basket) Oh! by the kestrels! I can keep my hands off you no longer; you are too slow and lazy altogether. (He hits Manes, who runs away. A young PARRICIDE enters.)

PARRICIDE: (singing) Oh! might I but become an eagle, who soars in the skies! Oh! might I fly above the azure waves of the barren sea!

PITHETAERUS: Ha! it would seem the news was true; I hear someone coming who talks of wings.

PARRICIDE: Nothing is more charming than to fly; I am bird-mad and fly towards you, for I want to live with you and to obey your laws.

PITHETAERUS: Which laws? The birds have many laws.

PARRICIDE: All of them; but the one that pleases me most is that among the birds it is considered a fine thing to peck and strangle one's father.

PITHETAERUS: Yes, by Zeus! according to us, he who dares to strike his father, while still a chick, is a brave fellow.

PARRICIDE: And therefore I want to dwell here, for I want to strangle my father and inherit his wealth.

PITHETAERUS: But we have also an ancient law written in the code of the storks, which runs thus, "When the stork father has reared his young and has taught them to fly, the young must in their turn support the father."

PARRICIDE: (petulantly) It's hardly worth while coming all this distance to be compelled to keep my father!

PITHETAERUS: No, no, young friend, since you have come to us with such willingness, I am going to give you these black wings, as though you were an orphan bird; furthermore, some good advice, that I received myself in infancy. Don't strike your father, but take these wings in one hand and these spurs in the other; imagine you have a cock's crest on your head and go and mount guard and

229

fight; live on your pay and respect your father's life. You're a gallant fellow! Very well, then! Fly to Thrace and fight.

PARRICIDE: By Bacchus! You're right; I will follow your counsel.

PITHETAERUS: It's acting wisely, by Zeus.

(The PARRICIDE departs, and the dithyrambic POET CINESIAS arrives.)

CINESIAS: (singing) "On my light pinions I soar off to Olympus; in its capricious flight my Muse flutters along the thousand paths of poetry in turn..."

PITHETAERUS: This fellow will need a whole shipload of wings.

CINESIAS: (singing) "...and being fearless and vigorous, it is seeking fresh outlet."

PITHETAERUS: Welcome, Cinesias, you lime-wood man! Why have you come here twisting your game leg in circles?

CINESIAS: (singing) "I want to become a bird, a tuneful nightingale."

PITHETAERUS: Enough of that sort of ditty. Tell me what you want.

CINESIAS: Give me wings and I will fly into the topmost airs to gather fresh songs in the clouds, in the midst of the vapours and the fleecy snow.

PITHETAERUS: Gather songs in the clouds?

CINESIAS: 'Tis on them the whole of our latter-day art depends. The most brilliant dithyrambs are those that flap their wings in empty space and are clothed in mist and dense obscurity. To appreciate this, just listen.

PITHETAERUS: Oh! no, no, no!

CINESIAS: By Hermes! but indeed you shall. (He sings.) "I shall travel through thine ethereal empire like a winged bird, who cleaveth space with his long neck..."

PITHETAERUS: Stop! Way enough!

CINESIAS: "...as I soar over the seas, carried by the breath of the winds..."

PITHETAERUS: By Zeus! I'll cut your breath short. (He picks up a pair of wings and begins trying to stop Cinesias' mouth with them.)

CINESIAS: (running away)"...now rushing along the tracks of Notus, now nearing Boreas across the infinite wastes of the ether." Ah! old man, that's a pretty and clever idea truly!

PITHETAERUS: What! are you not delighted to be cleaving the air?

CINESIAS: To treat a dithyrambic poet, for whom the tribes dispute with each other, in this style!

PITHETAERUS: Will you stay with us and form a chorus of winged birds as slender as Leotrophides for the Cecropid tribe?

CINESIAS: You are making game of me, that's clear; but know that I shall never leave you in peace if I do not have wings wherewith to traverse the air.

(CINESIAS: departs and an INFORMER: arrives.)

INFORMER: What are these birds with downy feathers, who look so pitiable to me? Tell me, oh swallow with the long dappled wings.

PITHETAERUS: Oh! it's a regular invasion that threatens us. Here comes another one, humming along.

INFORMER: Swallow with the long dappled wings, once more I summon you.

PITHETAERUS: It's his cloak I believe he's addressing; it stands in great need of the swallows' return.

INFORMER: Where is he who gives out wings to all comers?

PITHETAERUS: Here I am, but you must tell me for what purpose you want them.

INFORMER: Ask no questions. I want wings, and wings I must have.

PITHETAERUS: Do you want to fly straight to Pellene?

INFORMER: I? Why, I am an accuser of the islands, an Informer...

PITHETAERUS: A fine trade, truly!

INFORMER: ...a hatcher of lawsuits. Hence I have great need of wings to prowl round the cities and drag them before justice.

PITHETAERUS: Would you do this better if you had wings?

INFORMER: No, but I should no longer fear the pirates; I should return with the cranes, loaded with a supply of lawsuits by way of ballast.

PITHETAERUS: So it seems, despite all your youthful vigour, you make it your trade to denounce strangers?

INFORMER: Well, and why not? I don't know how to dig.

PITHETAERUS: But, by Zeus! there are honest ways of gaining a living at your age without all this infamous trickery.

INFORMER: My friend, I am asking you for wings, not for words.

PITHETAERUS: It's just my words that gives you wings.

INFORMER: And how can you give a man wings with your words?

PITHETAERUS: They all start this way.

INFORMER: How?

PITHETAERUS: Have you not often heard the father say to young men in the barbers' shops, "It's astonishing how Diitrephes' advice has made my son fly to horse-riding."-"Mine," says another, "has flown towards tragic Poetry on the wings of his imagination."

INFORMER: So that words give wings?

PITHETAERUS: Undoubtedly; words give wings to the mind and make a man soar to heaven. Thus I hope that my wise words will give you wings to fly to some less degrading trade.

INFORMER: But I do not want to.

PITHETAERUS: What do you reckon on doing then?

INFORMER: I won't belie my breeding; from generation to generation we have lived by informing. Quick, therefore, give me quickly some light, swift hawk or kestrel wings, so that I may summon the islanders, sustain the accusation here, and haste back there again on flying pinions.

PITHETAERUS: I see. In this way the stranger will be condemned even before he appears.

INFORMER: That's just it.

PITHETAERUS: And while he is on his way here by sea, you will be flying to the islands to despoil him of his property.

INFORMER: You've hit it, precisely; I must whirl hither and thither like a perfect humming-top.

PITHETAERUS: I catch the idea. Wait, I've got some fine Corcyraean wings. How do you like them?

INFORMER: Oh! woe is me! Why, it's a whip!

PITHETAERUS: No, no; these are the wings, I tell you, that make the top spin.

INFORMER: (as PITHETAERUS lashes him) Oh! oh! oh!

PITHETAERUS: Take your flight, clear off, you miserable cur, or you will soon see what comes of quibbling and lying.

(The INFORMER flees. To his slaves)

Come, let us gather up our wings and withdraw. (The baskets are taken away.)

CHORUS: (singing) In my ethereal flights I have seen many things new and strange and wondrous beyond belief. There is a tree called Cleonymus belonging to an unknown species; it has no heart, is good for nothing and is as tall as it is cowardly. In springtime it shoots forth calumnies instead of buds and in autumn it strews the ground with bucklers in place of leaves. Far away in the regions of darkness, where no ray of light ever enters, there is a country, where men sit at the table of the heroes and dwell with them always-except in the evening. Should any mortal meet the hero Orestes at night, he would soon be stripped and covered with blows from head to foot. (PROMETHEUS enters, masked to conceal his identity.)

PROMETHEUS: Ah! by the gods! if only Zeus does not espy me! Where is Pithetaerus?

PITHETAERUS: Ha! what is this? A masked man!

PROMETHEUS: Can you see any god behind me?

234

PITHETAERUS: No, none. But who are you, pray?

PROMETHEUS: What's the time, please?

PITHETAERUS: The time? Why, it's past noon. Who are you?

PROMETHEUS: Is it the fall of day? Is it no later than that?

PITHETAERUS: This is getting dull!

PROMETHEUS: What is Zeus doing? Is he dispersing the clouds or gathering them?

PITHETAERUS: Watch out for yourself!

PROMETHEUS: Come, I will raise my mask.

PITHETAERUS: Ah! my dear Prometheus!

PROMETHEUS: Sh! Sh! speak lower!

PITHETAERUS: Why, what's the matter, Prometheus?

PROMETHEUS: Sh! sh! Don't call me by my name; you will be my ruin, if Zeus should see me here. But, if you want me to tell you how things are going in heaven, take this umbrella and shield me, so that the gods don't see me.

PITHETAERUS: I can recognize Prometheus in this cunning trick. Come, quick then, and fear nothing; speak on.

PROMETHEUS: Then listen.

PITHETAERUS: I am listening, proceed!

PROMETHEUS: Zeus is done for.

PITHETAERUS: Ah! and since when, pray?

PROMETHEUS: Since you founded this city in the air. There is not a man who now sacrifices to the gods, the smoke of the victims no longer reaches us. Not the smallest offering comes! We fast as though it were the festivall of Demeter. The barbarian gods, who are dying of hunger, are bawling like Illyrians and threaten to make an armed descent upon Zeus, if he does not open markets where joints of the victims are sold.

PITHETAERUS: What! there are other gods besides you, barbarian gods who dwell above Olympus?

PROMETHEUS: If there were no barbarian gods, who would be the patron of Execestides?

PITHETAERUS: And what is the name of these gods?

PROMETHEUS: Their name? Why, the Triballi.

PITHETAERUS: Ah, indeed! 'tis from that no doubt that we derive the word 'tribulation.'

PROMETHEUS: Most likely. But one thing I can tell you for certain, namely, that Zeus and the celestial Triballi are going to send deputies here to sue for peace. Now don't you treat with them, unless Zeus restores the sceptre to the BIRDS: and gives you Basileia in marriage.

PITHETAERUS: Who is this Basileia?

PROMETHEUS: A very fine young damsel, who makes the lightning for Zeus; all things come from her, wisdom, good laws, virtue, the fleet, calumnies, the public paymaster and the triobolus.

PITHETAERUS: Ah! then she is a sort of general manageress to the god.

PROMETHEUS: Yes, precisely. If he gives you her for your wife, yours will be the almighty power. That is what I have come to tell you; for you know my constant and habitual goodwill towards men.

PITHETAERUS: Oh, yes! it's thanks to you that we roast our meat.

PROMETHEUS: I hate the gods, as you know.

PITHETAERUS: Aye, by Zeus, you have always detested them.

PROMETHEUS: Towards them I am a veritable Timon; but I must return in all haste, so give me the umbrella; if Zeus should see me from up there, he would think I was escorting one of the Canephori.

PITHETAERUS: ait, take this stool as well.

(PROMETHEUS leaves. PITHETAERUS goes into the thicket.)

CHORUS: (singing) Near by the land of the Sciapodes there is a marsh, from the borders whereof the unwashed Socrates evokes the souls of men. Pisander came one day to see his soul, which he had left there when still alive. He offered a little victim, a camel, slit his throat and, following the example of Odysseus, stepped one pace backwards. Then that bat of a Chaerephon came up from hell to drink the camel's blood.

(POSIDON enters, accompanied by HERACLES and TRIBALLUS.)

POSIDON: This is the city of Nephelococcygia, to which we come as ambassadors. (To TRIBALLUS) Hi! what are you up to? you are throwing your cloak over the left shoulder. Come, fling it quick over the right! And why, pray, does it draggle in this fashion? Have you ulcers to hide like Laespodias? Oh! democracy! whither, oh! whither are you leading us? Is it possible that the gods have chosen such an envoy? You are undisturbed? Ugh! you cursed savage! you are by far the most barbarous of all the gods.-Tell me, Heracles, what are we going to do?

HERACLES: I have already told you that I want to strangle the fellow who dared to wall us out.

POSIDON: But, my friend, we are envoys of peace.

HERACLES: All the more reason why I wish to strangle him.

(PITHETAERUS comes out of the thicket, followed by slaves, who are carrying various kitchen utensils; one of them sets up a table on which he places poultry dressed for roasting.)

PITHETAERUS: Hand me the cheese-grater; bring me the silphium for sauce; pass me the cheese and watch the coals.

HERACLES: Mortal! we who greet you are three gods.

PITHETAERUS: Wait a bit till I have prepared my silphium pickle.

HERACLES: What are these meats?

PITHETAERUS: These are birds that have been punished with death for attacking the people's friends.

HERACLES: And you are going to season them before answering us?

PITHETAERUS: (looking up from his work for the first time) Ah! Heracles! welcome, welcome! What's the matter?

POSIDON: The gods have sent us here as ambassadors to treat for peace.

PITHETAERUS: (ignoring this) There's no more oil in the flask.

HERACLES: And yet the birds must be thoroughly basted with it.

POSIDON: We have no interest to serve in fighting you;as for you, be friends and we promise that you shall always have rain-water in your pools and the warmest of warm weather. So far as these points go we are plenipotentiaries.

PITHETAERUS: We have never been the aggressors, and even now we are as well   disposed for peace as yourselves, provided you agree to one   equitable condition. namely, that Zeus yield his sceptre to the birds. If only this is agreed to, I invite the ambassadors to dinner.

HERACLES: That's good enough for me. I vote for peace.

POSIDON: You wretch! you are nothing but a fool and a glutton. Do you want to dethrone your own father?

PITHETAERUS: What an error. Why, the gods will be much more powerful if the birds govern the earth. At present the mortals are hidden beneath the clouds, escape your observation, and commit perjury in your name; but if you had the birds   for your allies, and a man, after having sworn by the crow and Zeus, should fail to keep his oath, the crow would dive down upon him unawares and pluck out his eye.

POSIDON: Well thought of, by Posidon!

HERACLES: My notion too.

PITHETAERUS: (to TRIBALLUS) And you, what's your opinion?

TRIBALLUS: Nabaisatreu.

PITHETAERUS: D'you see? he also approves. But listen, here is another thing in which we can serve you. If a man vows to offer a sacrifice to some god, and then procrastinates, pretending that the gods can wait, and thus does not keep his word, we shall punish his stinginess.

POSIDON: Ah! and how?

PITHETAERUS: While he is counting his money or is in the bath, a kite will relieve him, before he knows it, either in coin or in clothes, of the value of a couple of sheep, and carry it to the god.

HERACLES: I vote for restoring them the sceptre.

POSIDON: Ask Triballus.

HERACLES: Hi Triballus, do you want a thrashing?

TRIBALLUS: Sure, bashum head withum stick.

HERACLES: He says, "Right willingly."

POSIDON: If that be the opinion of both of you, why, I consent too.

HERACLES: Very well! we accord you the sceptre.

PITHETAERUS: Ah! I was nearly forgetting another condition. I will leave Here to Zeus, but only if the young Basileia is given me in marriage.

POSIDON: Then you don't want peace. Let us withdraw.

PITHETAERUS: It matters mighty little to me. Cook, look to the gravy.

HERACLES: What an odd fellow this Posidon is! Where are you off to? Are we going to war about a woman?

POSIDON: What else is there to do?

HERACLES: What else? Why, conclude peace.

POSIDON: Oh! you blockhead! do you always want to be fooled? Why, you are seeking your own downfall. If Zeus were to die, after having yielded them

240

the sovereignty, you would be ruined, for you are the heir of all the wealth he will leave behind.

PITHETAERUS: Oh! by the gods! how he is cajoling you. Step aside, that I may have a word with you. Your uncle is getting the better of you, my poor friend. The law will not allow you an obolus of the paternal property, for you are a bastard and not a legitimate child.

HERACLES: I a bastard! What's that you tell me?

PITHETAERUS: Why, certainly; are you not born of a stranger woman? Besides, is not Athene recognized as Zeus' sole heiress? And no daughter would be that, if she had a legitimate brother.

HERACLES: But what if my father wished to give me his property on his death-bed, even though I be a bastard?

PITHETAERUS: The law forbids it, and this same Posidon would be the first to lay claim to his wealth, in virtue of being his legitimate brother. Listen; thus runs Solon's law: "A bastard shall not inherit, if there are legitimate children; and if there are no legitimate children, the property shall pass to the nearest kin."

HERACLES: And I get nothing whatever of the paternal property?

PITHETAERUS: Absolutely nothing. But tell me, has your father had you entered on the registers of his phratry?

HERACLES: No, and I have long been surprised at the omission.

PITHETAERUS: Why do you shake your fist at heaven? Do you want to fight? Why, be on my side, I will make you a king and will feed you on bird's milk and honey.

HERACLES: Your further condition seems fair to me. I cede you the young damsel.

POSIDON: But I, I vote against this opinion.

PITHETAERUS: Then it all depends on the Triballus. (To the TRIBALLUS) What do you say?

TRIBALLUS: Givum bird pretty gel bigum queen.

HERACLES: He says give her.

POSIDON: Why no, he does not say anything of the sort, or else, like the swallows he does not know how to walk.

PITHETAERUS: Exactly so. Does he not say she must be given to the swallows?

POSIDON: (resignedly) All right, you two arrange the matter; make peace, since you wish it so; I'll hold my tongue.

HERACLES: We are of a mind to grant you all that you ask. But come up there with us to receive Basileia and the celestial bounty.

PITHETAERUS: Here are birds already dressed, and very suitable for a nuptial feast.

HERACLES: You go and, if you like, I will stay here to roast them.

PITHETAERUS: You to roast them? you are too much the glutton; come along with us.

HERACLES: Ah! how well I would have treated myself!

PITHETAERUS: Let some one bring me a beautiful and magnificent tunic for the wedding.

(The tunic is brought. PITHETAERUS and the three gods depart.)

CHORUS: (singing) At Phanae, near the Clepsydra, there dwells a people who have neither faith nor law, the Englottogastors, who reap, sow, pluck the vines and the figs with their tongues; they belong to a barbaric race, and among them the Philippi and the Gorgiases are to be found; 'tis these Englottogastorian Philippi who introduced the custom all over Attica of cutting out the tongue separately at sacrifices.

(A MESSENGER enters.)

MESSENGER: (in tragic style) Oh, you, whose unbounded happiness I cannot express in words, thrice happy race of airy birds, receive your king in your fortunate dwellings. More brilliant than the brightest star that illumes the earth, he is approaching his glittering golden palace; the sun itself does not shine with more dazzling glory. He is entering with his bride at his side, whose beauty no human tongue can express; in his hand he brandishes the lightning, the winged shaft of Zeus; perfumes of unspeakable sweetness pervade the ethereal realms. 'Tis a glorious spectacle to see the clouds of incense wafting in light whirlwinds before the breath of the zephyr! But here he is himself. Divine Muse! let thy sacred lips begin with songs of happy omen.

(PITHETAERUS enters, with a crown on his head; he is accompanied by BASILEIA.)

CHORUS: (singing) Fall back! to the right! to the left! advance! Fly around this happy mortal, whom Fortune loads with her blessings. Oh! oh! what grace! what beauty! Oh, marriage so auspicious for our city! All honour to this man! 'tis through him that the birds are called to such glorious destinies. Let your nuptial hymns, your nuptial songs, greet him and his Basileia! 'Twas in the midst of such festivities that the Fates formerly united Olympian Here to the King who governs the gods from the summit of his inaccessible throne. Oh! Hymen! oh! Hymenaeus! Rosy Eros with the golden wings held the reins and guided the chariot; 'twas he, who presided over the union of Zeus and the fortunate Here. Oh! Hymen! oh! Hymenaeus!

PITHETAERUS: I am delighted with your songs, I applaud your verses. Now celebrate the thunder that shakes the earth, the flaming lightning of Zeus and the terrible flashing thunderbolt.

CHORUS: (singing) Oh, thou golden flash of the lightning! oh, ye divine shafts of flame, that Zeus has hitherto shot forth! Oh, ye rolling thunders, that bring down the rain! 'Tis by the order of our king that ye shall now stagger the earth! Oh, Hymen! 'tis through thee that he commands the universe and that he makes Basileia, whom he has robbed from Zeus, take her seat at his side. Oh! Hymen! oh! Hymenaeus!

PITHETAERUS: (singing) Let all the winged tribes of our fellow-citizens follow the bridal couple to the palace of Zeus and to the nuptial couch! Stretch forth your hands, my dear wife! Take hold of me by my wings and let us dance; I am going to lift you up and carry you through the air.

(PITHETAERUS: and BASILEIA leave dancing; the CHORUS follows them.)

CHORUS: (singing) Alalai! Ie Paion! Tenilla kallinike! Loftiest art thou of gods!

THE END

Made in the USA
Charleston, SC
04 February 2013